SNAPSHOT

Elementary

Students'
Book

Brian Abbs

Ingrid Freebairn

Chris Barker

 LONGMAN

Contents

Vocabulary	Skills	Helpline	Soundbite
Countries and nationalities Family members Types of music	Speaking: see 'Communication' Listen to someone talking about her life Read about the city of Liverpool Write notes about a city in your country	Learning tips	/ sp / **Sp**ike / st / **St**ella / sk / **sch**ool
Parts of a room Furniture and objects Patterns and colours	Write a description of a room Read rules for a hostel	Organise new vocabulary (1)	Sentence stress: It's <u>on</u> the <u>floor</u>.
Revision			

Clock times
Periods of time
Free-time activities
	Read about a day in the life of a pop star
	  on tour
	Write about a typical week
	Listen to a telephone conversation
	  about a problem
		Test your memory	/ ps / sho**ps**
			/ ts / star**ts**
			/ ks / tal**ks**

Food and drink	Write a food diary Listen to a food programme Read about a day in the life of an animal film star	Organise new vocabulary (2)	/ tʃ / **ch**eese / dʒ / **j**uice
Revision			
Months and dates Sports Sports locations	Listen to a radio programme about future sporting events Read an interview with a footballer Write an interview with a sports star		/ θ / thir**d**, eigh**th**, nin**th**

Common adjectives
School subjects
	Read a ghost story
	Listen to a telephone conversation
	  about exam results
		Record past tense forms
		  of regular verbs
			/ t / stopp**ed**
			/ d / listen**ed**
			/ ɪd / start**ed**

Revision			
English money Places in towns	Read about The Beatles Listen to people buying things in a shop Listen to people giving directions	Learn past tense forms of irregular verbs	
Animals Rooms and parts of the house	Listen to a dialogue and note the correct order of events Read about a brave dog Write an animal story	Use a dictionary (1)	/ ɔː / h**or**se / ɒ / f**o**x
Revision			

Vocabulary	Skills	Helpline	Soundbite
Materials and personal possessions Clothes Physical description	Speaking: see 'Communication' Listen to a telephone conversation about a lost bag Read a message on the Internet Write a message on the Internet about a friend you want to contact	Learn by heart	/ h / have, haven't
Adjectives of measurement: *fast, heavy, high, long, wide*	Listen to a dialogue and answer questions Read about a theme park ride Write a postcard about an exciting ride	Check spelling	Sentence stress: It's the <u>longest</u> ride in the world.
Revision			
Parts of the body	Read and complete a questionnaire on good manners Write a Good Date Guide	Practise speaking	/ l / I'll, he'll
Household jobs Occupations	Read an article about helping in the house Listen to someone talking about an amusing incident	Improve your listening skills	Word stress: <u>doc</u>tor beau<u>ti</u>cian
Revision			

Vocabulary	Skills	Helpline	Soundbite
Leisure activities	Read *What's on?* advertisements Listen to a radio programme Write an invitation Read advice about how to be safe at carnivals	Use a dictionary (2)	/ aɪˈlaɪk / I like / aɪdˈlaɪk / I'd like
Adjectives and adverbs	Write a message of apology Listen to a dialogue and choose the best answers Read about voluntary work		Intonation in conditional sentences: If you go now, you'll have lots of time.
Revision	Revision		
Jobs in the media Types of films	Listen to an actor talking about acting in films Read about a popular film Write about a film you enjoyed	Reading in class	Fall–rise intonation: Don't worry, I won't.
Food and drink in a restaurant	Read about slavery Listen to a discussion about a museum	English outside the classroom	/ ə / was were
Revision			

Teen Work

Teen**Work** organises projects during the summer holidays for teenagers from all over the world.

The Liverpool Project

Location	Liverpool, England
Dates	3rd – 29th August
Accommodation	Hostel
The work	Community projects in Liverpool
Pay	No pay but free food and accommodation
Project leader	Mick Jordan

SCOTLAND
Edinburgh
NORTHERN IRELAND
Belfast
Dublin
EIRE
Liverpool
WALES
Cardiff
ENGLAND
London

The Liverpool Project volunteers *(from left to right)*

Joe Phillips from Manchester, UK; **Jennifer (Spike) Hunter** from Brighton, UK; **Sandra Mancuso** from Milan, Italy; **Gabriel Navarro** from Salamanca, Spain; **Louise Morgan** from London, UK; **Stefan Kowalski** from Cracow, Poland

The Liverpool Project staff *(from left to right)*

Mick Jordan, the project leader; **Stella Brennan**, the hostel warden, with her husband **David**, and children **Katie** and **Sam**

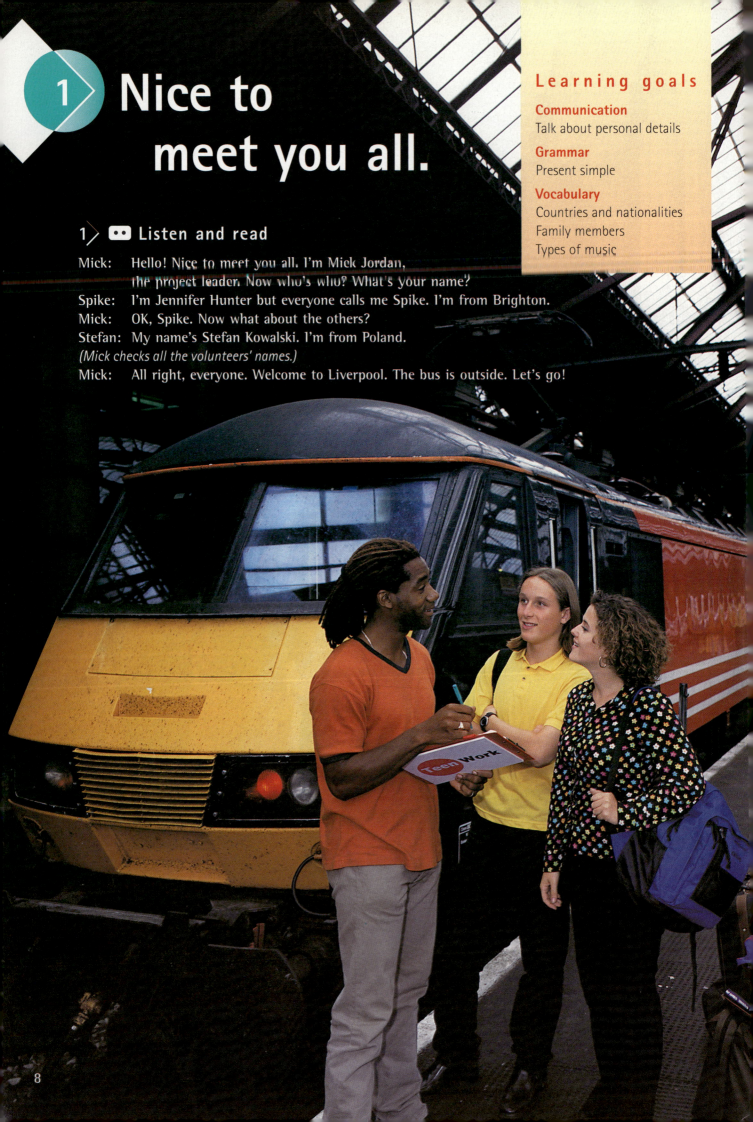

Learning goals

Communication
Talk about personal details

Grammar
Present simple

Vocabulary
Countries and nationalities
Family members
Types of music

1 Listen and read

Mick: Hello! Nice to meet you all. I'm Mick Jordan, the project leader. Now who's who? What's your name?

Spike: I'm Jennifer Hunter but everyone calls me Spike. I'm from Brighton.

Mick: OK, Spike. Now what about the others?

Stefan: My name's Stefan Kowalski. I'm from Poland.

(Mick checks all the volunteers' names.)

Mick: All right, everyone. Welcome to Liverpool. The bus is outside. Let's go!

2 > Comprehension

Answer T (true) or F (false).

1 All the volunteers are from England.
2 The volunteers are now in Liverpool.
3 Mick is one of the volunteers.
4 Spike's real name is Jennifer.
5 Mick checks the volunteers' addresses.

3 > Useful phrases

Listen and repeat.

- Nice to meet you all.
- Who's who?
- Everyone calls me [Spike].
- All right, everyone.
- Welcome to [Liverpool].
- Let's go!

```
P O L A N D N B Y
F B G R E E C E P
B R D G K M K T O
R A U E N R B U R
I Z I N U G D R T
T I I T A L Y K U
A L A I B E U E G
I C K N R H S Y A
N S P A I N Y T L
```

4 > Vocabulary

Countries and nationalities

a > Find nine countries in the word square and write them in a list with their nationality adjectives.

Country	Nationality
1 Poland	Polish

b > Add five more countries and nationalities to your list.

5 > Communication

Talking about personal details

▶ What's her name?
▶ It's Sandra.
▶ What nationality is she?
▶ She's Italian.
▶ Where's she from in Italy?
▶ She's from Milan.
▶ What's her surname?
▶ It's Mancuso.
▶ How do you spell that?
▶ M-A-N-C-U-S-O.

Now talk about three or four other people in the picture. Use the information on page 6 to help you.

6 > Over to you

Introduce yourself and say your name, nationality and where you are from. Or imagine you are one of the volunteers and introduce yourself.

Hello. My name's ... . I'm ... . I'm from ... .

7 > 🔢 Listen and read

That evening there is a welcome party at the hostel.

Stella: Hello, everyone! I'm Stella Brennan the hostel warden, and this is my husband, David. He teaches at the university.

David: Nice to meet you. Now, where do you all come from?

Later

Spike: Hello. Sorry I'm late! I'm Spike.

Katie: Spike? That's cool! I'm Katie. Sam! Turn the music down!

Spike: Who's Sam?

Katie: My brother. He likes techno music – but Mum doesn't!

Mick: Come over here, everybody! I want to take a photo of the group!

Spike: Oh, no! I hate group photos!

8 > Comprehension

Answer T (true) or F (false).

1 Stella is the hostel warden.
2 David is one of the volunteers.
3 Stella is Katie's mother.
4 Stella likes techno music.
5 Mick wants to take a photo of Stella.

9 > 🔢 Soundbite

The sounds / sp /, / st / and / sk /

Spike **St**ella **sk**ool
(Look at page 122.)

10 > Memory bank

Family members

List all the family words you know.

11 > Practice

Talk about the family relationship between:

• Stella • David • Katie
• Sam

Stella is David's wife.

12 > Over to you

Write about the people in your family.

Grammar snapshot

Present simple

Positive statements **Negative statements**
I come from Spain.   I don't come from Portugal.
He ... from Spain.   He ... come from Portugal.

Questions
Do you come from Spain?
Does he ... ?

Short answers
Positive   Negative
Yes, I do.   No, I ... .
Yes, he ... . No, he ... .

What are the missing words?

Make similar sentences using *she*, *we* and *they*.

13〉 Practice

a〉 👀 Look at the information about the Teen Work volunteers. Complete the conversation about Joe. Then listen and see if you were right.

A: Where ¹... Joe ²... from?
B: He ³... Manchester.
A: Oh, really? Where does he ⁴... in Manchester?
B: He ⁵... in a small house in the suburbs.
A: ⁶... his favourite school subject?
B: I think he likes Computer science.
A: What sort of music ⁷... he ⁸... ?
B: Well, he likes soul and jazz but he ⁹... pop very much.

b〉 Ask your partner about two other volunteers.

c〉 Interview two students in your class. Then make similar cards for them.

A: *Where do you come from?*
B: *I come from ... .*

14〉 👀 Listen

One of the volunteers is missing. Who is it? Listen and note the information for this person.

Teen Work — Joe Phillips
Town/City: Manchester
Home: Small house in the suburbs
Favourite school subject: Computer science
Music
– like: Soul, jazz
– not like: Pop

Teen Work — Gabriel Navarro
Town/City: Salamanca
Home: Small flat near the main square
Favourite school subject: Physics
Music
– like:
– not like: Heavy metal, Slow music

Teen Work — Spike Hunter
Town/City: Brighton
Home: House near the sea
Favourite school subject: Art
Music
– like: Reggae, rap
– not like: Country & western

Teen Work — Sandra Mancuso
Town/City: Milan
Home: Large flat in the north
Favourite school subject: English
Music
– like: Classical, pop
– not like: Heavy metal

Teen Work — Stefan Kowalski
Town/City: Cracow
Home: Flat in the centre
Favourite school subject: History
Music
– like: Spanish guitar music
– not like: Techno

Liverpool

Liverpool is a large city situated in the north-west of England on the River Mersey. It is a lively industrial, cultural and commercial centre and it has a ¹... of around 500,000 people.

In the past Liverpool was a large port. In the seventeenth and eighteenth centuries it was famous for its ²... with North America and Jamaica in sugar, cotton, tobacco and slaves.

In the nineteenth century it was the main port for millions of ³... to the USA from Britain, Scandinavia and Germany.

Welcome to Liverpool

Liverpool is an exciting place to visit with theatres, concert halls, ⁴..., clubs, restaurants and many other attractions. If you're interested in culture, the Albert Dock area contains a superb maritime ⁵..., a first-class art gallery and, of course, *The Beatles Story*, an exhibition which tells the story of Liverpool's most famous pop group. You can also take a ⁶... from the Albert Dock across the River Mersey.

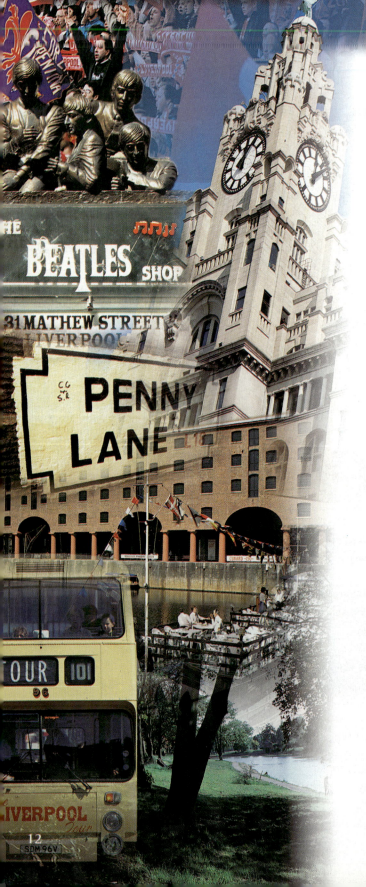

Before you read

What do the pictures tell you about Liverpool?

15 〉 Read

a〉 Read about the city of Liverpool and complete the texts with these words.

- cinemas • population • ferry • emigrants
- museum • trade

b〉 Copy and complete the notes about Liverpool.

1 Name of city: *Liverpool*
2 Location:
3 Type of city:
4 Population:
5 History:
    17th and 18th centuries: *Trade with ... in ...*
    19th century:
6 Tourist attractions:
7 Popular boat trip:

16 〉 Write and speak

Write similar notes about a big city in your country. Then tell the class about the city.

17 〉 **Help**line

Learning tips.

1 Ask your teacher about words you don't understand.
2 Write down all new words.
3 Repeat words or phrases when your teacher corrects you.
4 Speak in English as much as possible.
5 Always write out your homework corrections.

On the Mersey ferry

👀 Read the story and put the sentences at the bottom of the page in the correct places. Then listen and see if you were right.

Where is everybody?

1

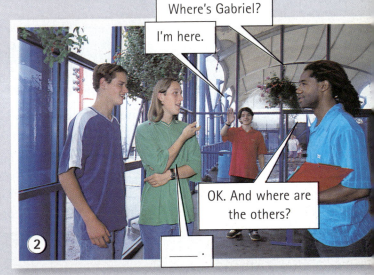

Where's Gabriel?

I'm here.

OK. And where are the others?

_____ .

2

Sorry I'm late.

That's all right. Where are Louise and Sandra?

They don't want to come. _____ .

OK. Come on. _____ . Let's get the ferry.

3

Where does the ferry go?

_____ . It's a very famous boat trip.

4

5

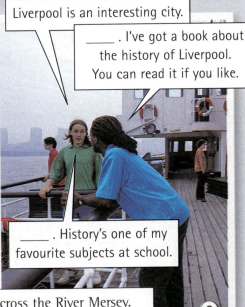

Liverpool is an interesting city.

_____ . I've got a book about the history of Liverpool. You can read it if you like.

_____ . History's one of my favourite subjects at school.

6

_____ and look at the view of the dock.

7

- Yes, it is. • Let's go! • It goes across the River Mersey.
- They don't like boats. • Come over here • Thank you.
- They aren't here yet.

13

2 You mustn't play loud music.

Learning goals

Communication
Talk about rules

Grammar
there is/there are with *some* and *any*
Verb *must/mustn't, can/can't*
Prepositions of place: *in, on, under, in front of, behind, above, next to, opposite, on the left/right (of), between, in the corner (of), near*

Vocabulary
Parts of a room
Furniture and objects
Patterns and colours

1 > Vocabulary Parts of a room, furniture and objects

Match the words with the items in the picture. *1- mirror*
Which items are not in the picture?

- bed • radio • table • lamp • wardrobe • mirror • carpet
- curtain • desk • washbasin • armchair • chair • radiator
- bookcase • wall • floor • wastepaper bin • posters • pictures
- door • noticeboard • window • duvet • cupboard

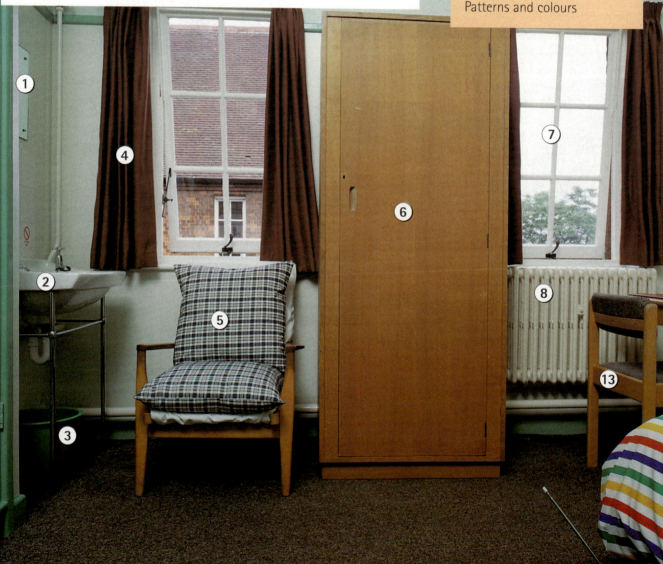

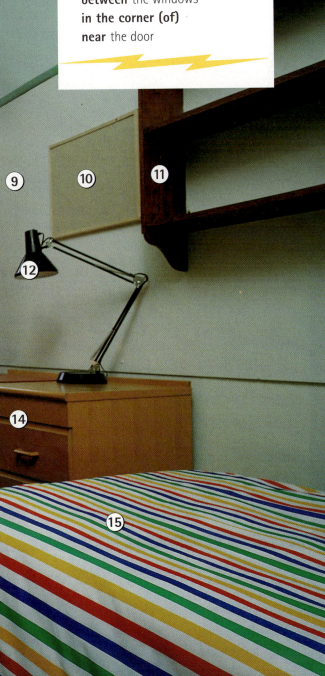

Grammar flash

Prepositions of place

in the cupboard
on the table
under the desk
in front of the radiator
behind the curtains
above the armchair
next to the table
opposite the bed
on the left/right (of)
between the windows
in the corner (of)
near the door

2 > Practice

Complete Spike's description of her room with the correct prepositions.

'My room at the hostel is a bit basic but it's OK. The walls are pale green and there are some plain brown curtains at the windows. ¹ *On the right* of the door there's a bed with a striped duvet. I keep my radio cassette player ²... the floor ³... the bed. There's a brown bookcase ⁴... the bed but there aren't any books ⁵... it! ⁶... the door there are two windows. ⁷... the windows there's a wardrobe. ⁸... the wardrobe, on the left, there's a blue and white checked armchair. ⁹... of the wardrobe there's a radiator ¹⁰... the window with a desk ¹¹... it. ¹²... of the room there's a washbasin. There's a mirror ¹³... the washbasin and a wastepaper bin ¹⁴... it. There aren't any pictures ¹⁵... the walls but there is a noticeboard ¹⁶... the desk. Oh, I forgot, there's also a plain brown carpet on the floor.'

3 > Soundbite   Sentence stress

It's <u>on</u> the <u>floor</u>. It's <u>under</u> the <u>desk</u>.
(Look at page 122.)

4 > Vocabulary

Patterns and colours

Describe the carpet, curtains and furniture, using the words below.

1 It's a green and yellow patterned carpet.

Patterns
• checked • patterned
• striped • spotted
• plain

Colours
• beige • black • blue
• brown • green • grey
• pink • purple • red
• white • yellow

Grammar snapshot

there is/there are with *some* and *any*

Positive statements
There's a desk in the room.
There ... ... posters above the bed.

Negative statements
There isn't a TV.
There ... ... pictures on the walls.

Questions
Is ... a washbasin in the room?
... ... books in the bookcase?

Short answers

Positive	Negative
Yes, ... is.	No, there ... .
Yes, there are.	No, there ... .

What are the missing words?

5 Practice

Test your memory. Ask and answer about the things in Spike's room on pages 14 and 15.

- desk • wardrobe • posters • carpet • radio
- sofa • bookcase • TV • washbasin • table
- cupboard • lamp • mirror • pictures • vase
- armchair • chair • books • wastepaper bin

A: *Is there a desk in Spike's room?*
B: *Yes, there is. It's next to the window.*
A: *Are there any pictures on the walls?*
B: *No, there aren't.*

6 Interaction

Students A and B

- Draw an outline of your room at home. Draw the bed and mark where the doors and windows are.
- Exchange outlines with your partner.
- Take turns to ask questions and complete the plan of your partner's room.

7 Write

Write a description of your room.

I (don't) like my room. It's quite/very small. I share it with my brother. The walls are ... . There's a plain red ... and there are some ...

8 👀 Listen and read

Mick: Hi! How's it going? How do you like your rooms?
Spike: They're a bit basic but they're OK.
Mick: You can put some posters on the walls if you like but you mustn't use drawing pins.
Spike: Can we move the furniture around?
Mick: Yes, if you want to. Hey, I like your guitar, Stefan.
Stefan: It's a present from my uncle.
Mick: Don't forget that you mustn't play loud music after ten thirty at night.
Spike: Yes, we know.

9 Comprehension

Correct the sentences.

Spike thinks the rooms are brilliant.
Spike thinks the rooms are basic.

1 There are some pictures on the walls.
2 They can't change anything in the room.
3 The guitar is Stefan's uncle's.
4 They can play loud music until eleven o'clock.

must/mustn't, can/can't
(I, you, he, she, it, we, they)

You **must** be quiet after 10.30.
You **mustn't** play loud music after 10.30.
You **can** put some posters on the walls.
You **can't** make coffee in your room.

11 Practice

a) **Talk about your school rules with** *can/can't* **or** *must/mustn't.*

1 We can use calculators in Maths exams.
2 We mustn't chew gum in class.

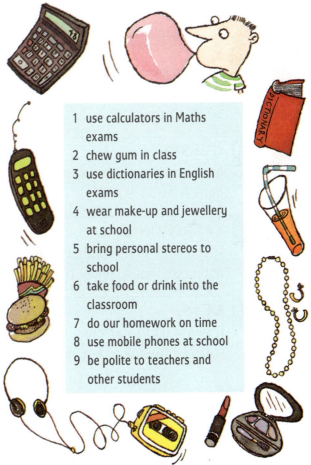

1 use calculators in Maths exams
2 chew gum in class
3 use dictionaries in English exams
4 wear make-up and jewellery at school
5 bring personal stereos to school
6 take food or drink into the classroom
7 do our homework on time
8 use mobile phones at school
9 be polite to teachers and other students

b) **Write two more school rules.**

10 Useful phrases

Listen and repeat.

- How's it going?
- [You can …] if you like.
- Yes, if you want to.
- Hey!
- Don't forget that …

12 Helpline

Organise new vocabulary (1).

1 Write down new words in a separate notebook.
2 Where possible, organise your vocabulary in word groups, e.g. furniture, patterns, colours.

HOSTEL RULES

1 ROOM DECORATION
You can put posters and photographs on the walls of your bedroom, but please do not use drawing pins.

2 FOOD AND DRINK
You can make tea, coffee and light snacks in the kitchen, but please do not take food into the bedrooms.

3 RADIOS AND SOUND SYSTEMS
You can have radios and sound systems in your rooms, but please do not play loud music after 10.30 p.m.

4 GUESTS
You can have guests in your rooms, but they must leave by 9 p.m.

5 TELEPHONES
If you want to make phone calls, please use the public pay phone under the stairs in the hall.

6 KEYS
If you want to stay out after 10 p.m., you must collect a front door key from the office.

24 Hour Minicab

ONARCH

Number 1 for Service

37

FREE HOME DELIVERY

GREAT WALL

Peking and Cantonese Takeaway

13 > Read

Read the hostel rules. Find the rule which gives information about:

a) inviting friends into your room.
b) putting things on bedroom walls.
c) coming in late.
d) making phone calls.
e) making snacks.
f) playing music.

14 > Communication

Talking about rules

▶ Can I put posters on the wall?
▶ Yes, you can if you like, but you mustn't use drawing pins.
▶ Can I make coffee in my room?
▶ No, I'm afraid you can't. You must use the kitchen.

Use the questions to make conversations about the hostel rules.

1 put posters on the wall?
2 make coffee in my room?
3 play my sound system?
4 make phone calls?
5 have friends in my room?
6 stay out late at night?

15 > Over to you

Tell the class about any rules you have at home for:

• using the phone.
• playing music.
• watching TV.
• having friends round.
• going out in the evening.

Do you think any of these rules are unfair?

 # Fast rewind UNITS 1 and 2

Grammar

1> Choose the correct part of the verb *to be* to complete the sentences.

... you American?   a) Am   b) <u>Are</u>   c) Is

1 Stefan and Gabriel ... both volunteers.
   a) is   b) are   c) be
2 A: Are you from Spain? B: Yes, I ... .
   a) am   b) is   c) are
3 Joe ... American, he's English.
   a) aren't   b) isn't   c) am
4 His name's Sam and ... Katie's brother.
   a) he   b) is   c) he's
5 They ... Joe's bags, they're Spike's.
   a) aren't   b) are   c) isn't
6 Spike ... not her real name.
   a) it's   b) is   c) it

2> Complete the sentences with the correct form of the verb(s) in brackets.

She ... coffee. (not like)   *She doesn't like coffee.*
1 ... you ... in Liverpool? (live)
2 He ... from Poland. (come)
3 I ... the guitar. (play)
4 We ... her Spike. (call)
5 What ... your mother ...? (want)
6 My parents ... my sort of music. (not like)
7 ... all the students ... from Spain? (come)

3> Complete the text with *can*, *must* or *mustn't*.

'My school is a girls' boarding school. We live at school and there are lots of rules. Everyone [1] *must* wear a white blouse and a grey skirt. The blouse [2] ... have long sleeves and the skirt [3] ... be too short. We [4] ... wear make-up in school but we [5] ... wear lipstick in the evening. At weekends we [6] ... go into town but we [7] ... be back by nine o'clock. Of course, we [8] ... go into bars or restaurants – that's against the rules.'

4> Complete the sentences with the correct form of *there is* or *there are*.

It's a big house. *There are* six bedrooms altogether.

1 In my room ... a desk next to the bed.
2 ... some posters on the wall and ... also a big mirror.
3 A: ... a phone in your room?
   B: No, ... , but ... one downstairs in the hall.
4 A: ... any good shops near your home?
   B: Yes, ... some quite good ones.
5 I like London because ... lots of parks and trees.

Vocabulary

5> Choose the odd word in each group.

	Italian	<u>Britain</u>	Spanish	French
1	science	classical	rap	reggae
2	yellow	plain	blue	grey
3	brother	father	girl	daughter
4	black	checked	patterned	striped
5	bedroom	dining room	garden	kitchen
6	carpet	hall	mirror	wardrobe
7	shower	bath	sitting room	washbasin

Communication

6> Work in pairs. Student A:
Ask Student B
• what his/her name and address is.
• how many brothers and sisters he/she has got.
• what sort of music he/she likes and doesn't like.
• to describe his/her bedroom at home.

Now Student B:
Ask Student A
• what his/her telephone number is.
• how many nationalities there are in the class.
• what school subjects he/she likes and doesn't like.
• to describe his/her sitting room at home.

Progress update Units 1 and 2
How do you rate your progress? Tick the chart.

	Excellent ★★★★	Good ★★★	OK ★★	Can do better ★
Grammar				
Vocabulary				
Communication				

I always have coffee.

Before you read

What do you think rock stars do every day?
What do they eat?
How do they travel about?

1 > Read

Rocking around the clock:
On tour with Jon Bon Jovi

Bon Jovi is one of the biggest rock bands in the world. Rick Stevens joins the lead singer and actor Jon Bon Jovi on the day of an important show.

I always have coffee

Jon usually gets up between nine and ten in the morning. It depends how tired he is. 'I'm never at my best first thing in the morning so I always have lots of coffee for breakfast,' says Jon. 'I really need it.'

Jon likes to keep fit. 'I go to the gym four mornings a week and do weightlifting,' he says. 'I also run for about half an hour in the evening.'

Jon has lunch at one o'clock. He prefers ordinary Italian or American food. He eats a lot of junk food and he never diets.

In the afternoon he gives interviews. There are lots of journalists who want to interview him so he sometimes gives six or seven interviews in a day.

On the road

The members of the Bon Jovi rock band usually travel to and from their gigs in minibuses. The windows are dark so people can't see them. 'People always get excited when they see us and we don't want any car accidents.'

When they travel long distances, they go by helicopter or plane. 'People think that's exciting, but it's not. Airports are boring places.'

Show time

At ten o'clock it's time for Bon Jovi to go out on stage and start their show. Their concerts last about two hours. After the show they usually go to a restaurant and relax. 'We're always on a high after a gig, so we don't go straight to bed!'

2> Comprehension

Read the article about Bon Jovi again and correct the notes.

1 Jon gets up at eight o'clock in the morning.
No, he doesn't. He gets up between nine and ten.

Jon Bon Jovi on tour

1 Jon gets up at eight o'clock in the morning.
2 He always has tea in the morning.
3 He swims to keep fit.
4 He doesn't like junk food.
5 He doesn't give many interviews.
6 The band usually start their show early in the evening.
7 After the show they usually go back to their hotel to sleep.

3> Memory bank

Clock times

Match the time phrases below with the points on the clock.

A – o'clock

- ten past
- twenty to
- o'clock
- quarter past
- quarter to
- half past

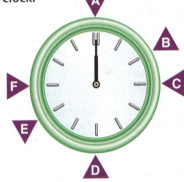

Periods of time

Complete the missing numbers.

15 minutes = a quarter of an hour
1 ... minutes = half an hour
2 ... minutes = three quarters of an hour
3 ... minutes = an hour

4> Over to you

Answer the questions.

What's the time now?
What time do you start school?
What time do you finish school?
How long is your lunch break?
How long is your English lesson?

Grammar snapshot

Adverbs of frequency

• usually • often • always • never • sometimes

I **always** have lots of coffee in the morning.
He is **often** tired in the morning.

Put the adverbs in order of frequency starting with *always.*

Phrases of frequency

How often do you see your grandmother? I see her **once / twice a week.**
How often do you go to the cinema? I go **three times a month.**

Make rules using *before* **or** *after.*

1 Adverbs of frequency come ... the main verb but ... the verb *to be.*
2 Phrases of frequency come ... the verb (and the object).

5 Practice

Complete the sentences about Bon Jovi's day with *always, never, usually* **or** *sometimes* **and the correct form of the verb.**

He (get up) ... between nine and ten o'clock.
He usually gets up between nine and ten o'clock.

1 He (be) ... very lively first thing in the morning.
2 He (drink) ... lots of coffee when he wakes up.
3 He (go) ... to the gym in the morning.
4 He (give) ... six or seven interviews in the afternoon.
5 He (eat) ... what he likes.
6 The band (travel) ... by bus between gigs.
7 They (go to bed) ... straight after a show.

6 Soundbite

The sounds / ps /, / ts / and / ks /
shops   starts   talks
(Look at page 122.)

7 Communication

Talking about routines

▶ What do you do after school?
▶ I usually do my homework but I sometimes play football. What do you do?
▶ I usually go straight home and watch TV.
▶ Do you ever go to the cinema?
▶ Yes, I do.
▶ How often do you go?
▶ Once a week, usually on Saturday.

Talk about what you do after school and at the weekend. Use these prompts to help you.

• go to a football match
• rent a video • visit relatives
• go to the cinema • write letters
• watch TV • visit friends
• play video games • play football
• go to a disco • listen to a CD
• go to the gym • do homework
• surf the Internet

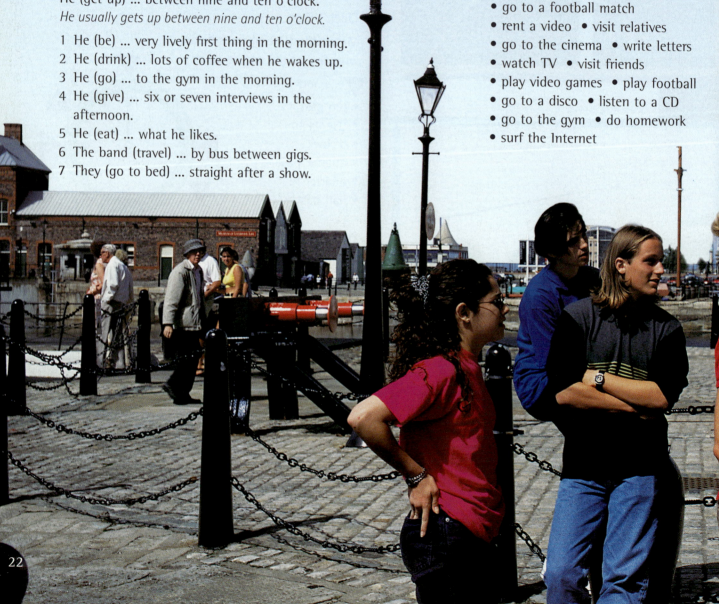

8 Write

Write about a typical week in your life. Or imagine a day in the life of a famous person and write about it.

9 🔊 Listen and read

Man: Excuse me, I'm looking for Albert Dock.

Spike: It's over there. I'm going there myself.

Man: Oh, really? Do you work there?

Spike: Yes. I'm working on a project. We're helping to make a youth centre.

Later

Mick: Good afternoon, Spike!

Spike: That's not fair! I'm only a few minutes late.

Mick: OK. This is the routine, everybody. We usually work from nine o'clock – or in Spike's case nine fifteen – to three thirty but today we're only working until three.

Spike: Good!

10 Comprehension

Answer the questions.

1 Where does the man want to go?
2 What work are the volunteers doing?
3 How late is Spike?
4 What are the normal hours of work?
5 What's different about today?

11 🔊 Useful phrases

Listen and repeat.

- Excuse me.
- Oh, really?
- That's not fair!
- Good!

Grammar snapshot

Present continuous

Positive statements
I'm staying in a hostel.

Negative statements
I'm not staying at a hotel.

Questions
... you staying in a hostel?
Is he ... in a hostel?

Short answers

Positive	Negative
Yes, I am.	No, I ... .
Yes, he	No, he ... .

What are the missing words?

Go back and look.
Find more examples of the present continuous in the dialogue.

12 Practice

Use the cues to write sentences in the present continuous.

1 Who (you/write to) ... ?
2 The volunteers (stay) ... in a hostel.
3 Their records (not/sell) ... very well in the USA.
4 (your brother/study) ... at university now?
5 Louise (not/feel) ... very well at the moment.

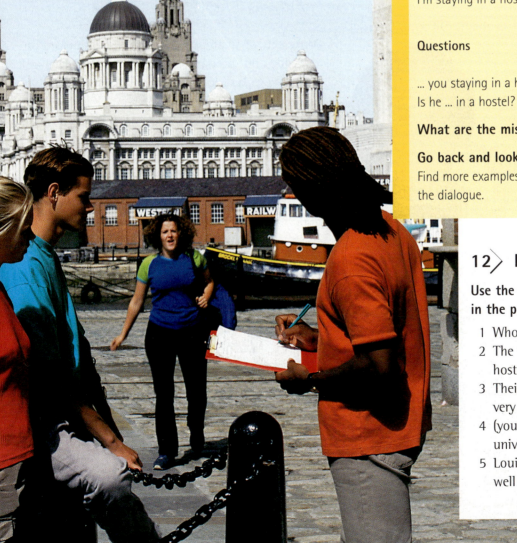

⚡ Grammar flash ⚡

Present simple and continuous in contrast

We usually **work** from 9 o'clock to 3.30 but today we**'re working** until 3.00.

I **live** in Salamanca but at the moment I**'m staying** in Liverpool.

Make rules.

1 We use the ... for daily routines and fixed times.

2 We use the ... for activities which are happening at the time of speaking or for a limited period of time.

13 〉 Practice

Look at the pictures of famous people. What's strange about them? Make sentences using these verbs.

- act - play - sing

1 *In the picture Leonardo DiCaprio is singing but he usually acts in films.*

14 〉 Over to you

Talk about:

- the books you usually read. Then say what you are reading at the moment.
- the clothes you usually wear. Then say what you are wearing at the moment.
- the topics you're studying in History and Geography this term.

15 〉 ⊙ Listen

Listen to the telephone conversation between Louise and her mother and answer the questions.

1 What is Louise doing when her mother phones?

2 What's the news about her father?

3 When is Louise's mother going to phone again?

16 〉 **Help**line

Test your memory.

to interview   excited   to relax

to depend   journalist   to diet

Make sets of small cards with the English word on one side and the translation on the other. Then ask someone to test you.

1 Leonardo DiCaprio (films)

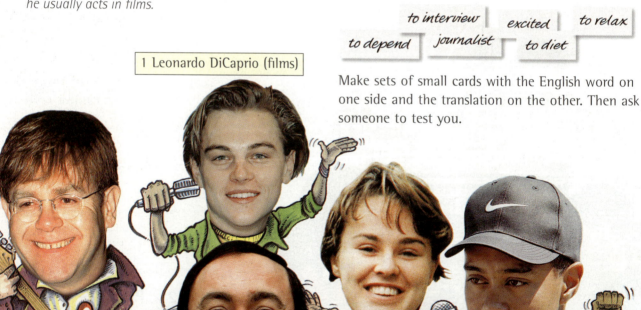

2 Elton John (piano)

3 Pavarotti (opera)

4 Martina Hingis (tennis)

5 Tiger Woods (golf)

At the hostel after work

Read the story and put the questions at the bottom of the page in the correct places. Then listen and see if you were right.

- Who from?
- What's the time?
- What are you two doing?
- What are all the others doing?
- What's the matter with Louise?
- How's it going?
- Well, does he still love you?

25

4 ▷ Would you like a sandwich?

Learning goals

Communication
Offer food and drink with *would like*

Grammar
Countable and uncountable nouns
Verb *have got* with *some* and *any*
going to future

Vocabulary
Food and drink

1 ▷ Vocabulary

Food and drink

Look at the pictures and match the words with the numbers.

- apple • yoghurt • bread
- cheese • pasta • egg
- beef • onion • peas
- butter • nuts • milk
- orange • lamb • fish
- lettuce • carrot
- potato • doughnut
- banana • tomato
- biscuit • olive oil
- cucumber • beans
- rice • lemon
- mushroom
- chicken
- cake
- melon
- peach

Grammar flash

Countable and uncountable nouns

Countable nouns have a plural form

Singular	Plural
one banana	two bananas

Uncountable nouns have only one form

coffee   tea   money

I like **coffee** but I don't like **tea**.

Grammar snapshot

Verb *have got* **with** *some* **and** *any*

Positive statements
I've got some eggs.
She ... some coffee.

Negative statements
I haven't got any biscuits.
She ... got any fruit.

Questions

... you got any potatoes?
... she got any milk?

Short form answers

Positive	Negative
Yes, I have.	No, I ... .
Yes, she	No, she ... .

What are the missing words?

Note.
We use *some* and *any* with both uncountable and plural countable nouns.

2 > Practice

a> Say which of these words are countable (C) and which are uncountable (U).

apple C   butter U

- apple • butter • bread • doughnut
- rice • olive oil • spaghetti • biscuit
- beef

b> Which of these foods are good/not good for you? Think about:

- carbohydrates • proteins • fats • vitamins

3 > Helpline

Organise new vocabulary (2).

A helpful way to learn words which belong to a large group is to make a word web.

Copy the word web and add the food words from this unit.

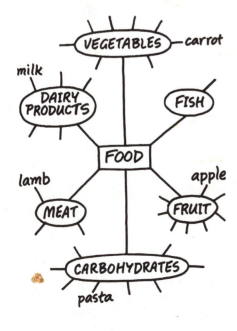

4 > Interaction

Student B: Turn to page 121.
Student A: You are at a supermarket. You want to make a cheese omelette and a mixed salad for lunch. Look at the recipe and phone Student B to ask if the things you need are in the kitchen. Then make a list of things you must buy.

A: *I want to make a cheese omelette and a mixed salad for lunch. Have we got any eggs?*
B: *No, we haven't.*
A: *Have we got any ... ?*

Cheese omelette

Ingredients
eggs, butter, cheese, salt, pepper

Mixed salad

Ingredients
lettuce, tomatoes, cucumber, oil, vinegar, salt, pepper

5 > Over to you

Write a food diary by making a note of everything you eat and drink during one day. Then compare your diary with your friend's diary. How healthy is your diet?

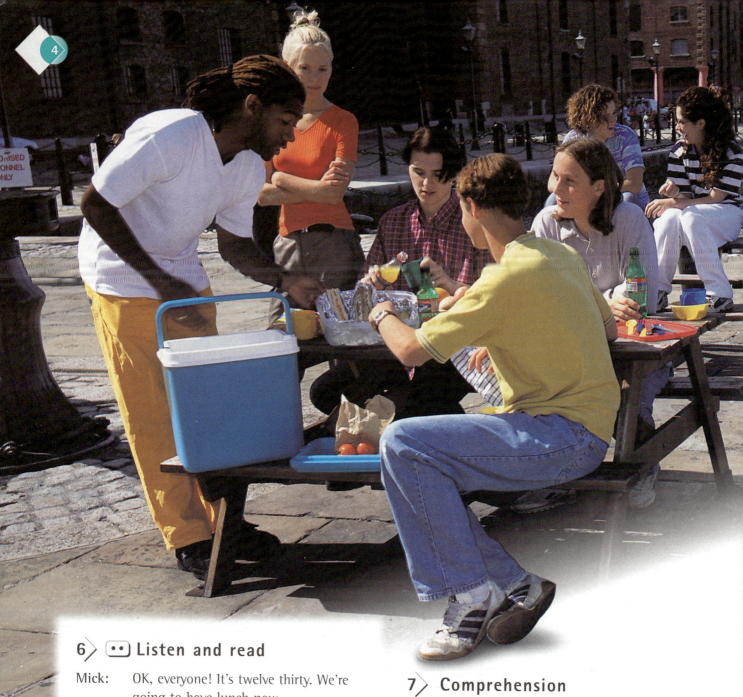

6 Listen and read

Mick: OK, everyone! It's twelve thirty. We're going to have lunch now.

Joe: Great! I'm starving.

Mick: Help yourselves to sandwiches. We've got chicken, tuna, or cheese and tomato. What would you like, Joe?

Joe: I'd like chicken, please.

Mick: What about you, Louise? What are you going to have?

Louise: Nothing, thanks. I'm not hungry.

Mick: Would you like some fruit?

Louise: No, thanks.

Later

Mick: All right, everyone. It's time to start work again.

Gabriel: What are we going to do this afternoon, Mick?

Mick: Clear the yard.

Gabriel: Must we? It's so hot and sunny.

Mick: Sorry, Gabriel. We're here to work!

7 Comprehension

a Answer these questions.

1 When do they have lunch?
2 What sort of sandwiches are there?
3 Is Louise hungry?

b Answer T (true), F (false) or DK (don't know).

1 Joe is hungry.
2 There aren't any sandwiches for vegetarians.
3 There are two sorts of fruit.
4 The weather is fine and sunny.

8 Useful phrases

Listen and repeat.

- Great!
- I'm starving.
- Help yourself/yourselves to [sandwiches].
- It's time to [start work again].

Grammar snapshot

going to **future**

Positive statements
We're going to have lunch.

Negative statements
We aren't ... have a big lunch.

Yes/No questions

... we ... have lunch?

Short form answers
Positive   Negative
Yes, we ... .   No, we ... .

What are the missing words?

9 〉 ⊡ Sound**bite**

The sounds / tʃ / and / dʒ /

cheese **ch**ips **j**uice **j**am
(Look at page 122.)

10 〉 Communication

Offering food and drink

▶ Would you like a sandwich?
▶ Yes, please.
▶ What sort would you like?
▶ I'd like chicken, please.
▶ OK. Help yourself. Would you like something to drink?
▶ Yes, please. Have you got any diet coke?

Later.

▶ Would you like another sandwich?/some more coke?
▶ Yes, please./No, thanks. I'm fine.

Choose two of the situations and offer your partner things to eat and drink.

• after school at your house
• at a class party • at a picnic

11 〉 Practice

Complete the dialogue with the correct form of *going to* **and the verb in brackets.**

Mother: Well, we (watch) ¹ ... a video. (you/join) ² ... us, Gary?

Gary: No, thanks. I (see) ³ ... if Russ is in.

Mother: But he lives on the other side of town. How (you/get) ⁴ ... there?

Gary: I (cycle) ⁵ ... . It's not that far!

Mother: Well, take your anorak. I think it (rain) ⁶ ... .

Gary: OK, OK! See you later!

12 〉 ⊡ Listen

a〉 Listen to Michelle, Cindy and Jack talking about what they're going to have for lunch today. Complete the lists.

Michelle: *plain yoghurt, ...*
Cindy: *an egg and tomato sandwich, ...*
Jack: *a slice of pizza, ...*

b〉 Which person is going to have a healthy lunch?

My day – by Cheetah the chimpanzee

Name : Cheetah
Home: Palm Springs, California, USA
Reason for fame: star of 50 Hollywood films, including 18 *Tarzan* films with Johnny Weissmuller
Best human friend: Dan Westfall

A After dinner I relax. I listen to the radio or watch old videos of myself in *Tarzan* films with Johnny Weissmuller. This evening I'm going to watch a wildlife film. It's a good life.

B I have afternoon tea at about 4 o'clock. I usually have a banana but this afternoon, for a special treat, Dan is going to take me down the freeway to a hamburger restaurant. After tea I do some abstract painting.

C In the morning I hang out in my room. I've got a TV, radio, air-conditioning and a fridge. Lunch is between 12 and 2 p.m. I try to eat healthy food. Today I'm going to have some fruit and a raw onion.

D In the afternoon I often go out with Dan. I ride on the back of his Honda scooter. People stop and stare at us. I don't know why. I make faces and wave to other drivers.

E Dinner is between 6 p.m. and 8 p.m. I have rice or spaghetti with tomato sauce or macaroni cheese. Most chimpanzees are vegetarian but I eat anything.

F I usually wake up between 6 a.m. and 7 a.m. and have a really good scratch. I don't wear any clothes unless someone is going to take my photograph. Dan, my human friend, takes me to breakfast at 8 o'clock. It's usually muesli with milk and sugar.

13 Read

a Read the text and rearrange the paragraphs in the correct order.

b Guess the meaning of these words and phrases.

- scratch • human • hang out • raw • stare
- make faces • wave • treat • abstract

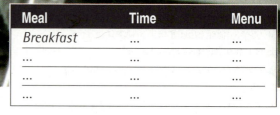

Meal	Time	Menu
Breakfast	...	...
...	...	...
...	...	...
...	...	...

c Copy and complete the chart above about Cheetah's meals.

d Answer the questions.

What's surprising about Cheetah's:
- room? • diet? • free-time activities?

14 Write

Imagine you are an animal. Write about a day in your life.

Fast rewind UNITS 3 and 4

Grammar

1 Complete the sentences with the correct form of the verb in brackets and write the times in words.

I ... at 7.30 in the morning. (get up)
I get up at half past seven in the morning.

1 She always ... to school by bus. (travel)
2 He usually ... from 8 a.m. until 4 p.m. (work)
3 Carla ... lunch at school. (not have)
4 They ... home from college until 4.15. (not get)
5 He sometimes ... to French classes on Monday. (go)
6 ... she always ... her homework on the bus? (do)
7 The film ... until 8.50. (not start)
8 ... you usually ... before you go to sleep? (read)

2 Choose the correct tense: present simple or present continuous.

Karen *walks/is walking* to school every day.

1 Jack's in the gym. He *plays/is playing* basketball.
2 Louise *likes/is liking* ballet music very much.
3 Sarah *does/is doing* gymnastics every Thursday evening.
4 Sam and Katie *have/are having* a tennis lesson at the moment.
5 Joe usually *runs/is running* round the park every evening.

3 Complete the sentences with *some* or *any*.

A: Have you got ¹*any* ice cream?
B: Yes, there's ²... vanilla ice cream in the fridge.
A: Is there ³... milk?
B: No, but I've got ⁴... cream.
A: That's fine. Are there ⁵... strawberries?
B: No, but there are ⁶... bananas.
A: That's no good. I need ⁷... strawberries.
B: Why?
A: Because I want to make a strawberry milkshake.

4 Complete the sentences with the correct form of the *going to* future.

They ... across the USA next year. (drive)
They're going to drive across the USA next year.

1 She ... in Ireland next year. (study)
2 We ... in a hotel. (not stay) We ... . (camp)
3 How long ... in Australia? (you and your family/be)
4 I'm ... you the answers. (not tell)
5 Spike's parents ... her next week. (visit)
6 ... the football final on TV? (you/watch)

Vocabulary

5 Choose the correct ending to complete the food words.

• ato • ese • nge • ter • ken • ad • tuce • on

1 butter

1 but	3 let	5 che	7 ora
2 oni	4 pot	6 chic	8 bre

Communication

6 Reorder the sentences to complete the conversation.

A: *Would you like something to drink?*
B: *Yes, please.*

a) Sure. What sort would you like?
b) What sort have you got?
c) I'd like a glass of fruit juice, please.
d) No, thanks. This is fine.
e) Orange and apple.
f) Here you are. Would you like some ice?
g) I'd like orange, please.
h) What would you like? There's fruit juice, tea, coffee or mineral water.

7 Work in pairs. Student A:
Ask Student B
• what time he/she usually gets up.
• what his/her mother or father is doing at this moment.
• what he/she is going to do at the weekend.

Now Student B:
Ask Student A
• what time he/she usually goes to bed.
• what your teacher is doing at the moment.
• what he/she is going to do after school.

Progress update Units 3 and 4

How do you rate your progress? Tick the chart.

	Excellent ★★★★	Good ★★★	OK ★★	Can do better ★
Grammar				
Vocabulary				
Communication				

Radio Days

Helen Bowen goes to interview Britain's youngest disc jockeys.

Rowan Muir and Rowan Bates-Hamilton, both aged fifteen, live in Ullapool, a fishing port on the north-west coast of Scotland. The girls are Britain's youngest disc jockeys. They present their own radio show, *Kids OK?* every Saturday morning from eleven to twelve midday on the local radio station, Lochbroom FM.

Rowan Muir is the programme presenter and her school friend, 'Rowan Two', is her co-presenter. Lochbroom FM is now one of the top community radio stations in the UK.

People come from all over the world to see how the radio station works. 'At this very moment, a TV crew from Japan are making a film about the girls,' says station manager, Steve Boyle.

Do local teenagers like the programme? Rowan Muir says, 'All the girls at school like it. The boys were silly about it at first, but now they're asking us to play their favourite records, so it must be OK.'

The two girls usually write all their scripts and choose the music. 'We always do a special five-minute feature on one particular artist or group. Today we're doing one on Queen. Next week we're going to do a programme on Oasis and Blur.'

There is one problem with Lochbroom FM: the FM signal is weak. 'Only about 5,000 people can hear our programme, and so I'm afraid you must travel to the top of north-west Scotland to hear us,' says Rowan Muir. 'But that's cool. Small is beautiful!'

Before you read

What's your favourite radio programme?
What sort of music is played on it?

1 〉 Read

a) Read about Lochbroom FM and guess the meaning of these words. Check your answers with your teacher or dictionary.

- disc jockey
- fishing port
- TV crew
- station manager
- script
- (special) feature
- particular

b) Complete the programme notes about Lochbroom FM.

Name of radio station:	Presenters:
Location:	Today's special feature:
Programme title:	Next week's special feature:
Starts at:	Size of audience:
Finishes at:	

2 〉 Speak

In pairs or groups, plan a programme for your local radio station. Then tell the class about your programme.

3 〉 Write

Read the letter from a girl who listens to *Kids OK?*. Write a similar letter to a disc jockey (DJ) at your favourite radio station.

Ullapool

SCOTLAND

Write the name and address of the person you are writing to.

The presenters,
Lochbroom FM.
Ullapool
IV26 2TS

Write your address here.

12 Rosebank Terrace,
Ullapool
IV26 5RP

Write the date here.

2nd August

Begin your letter like this.

Dear Rowan and Rowan,

Say who you are and introduce the subject.

My name is Caroline Taggart. I'm 14 years old and I live in Ullapool. I really like your programme. My friend and I listen to it every Saturday. I like the records you play and also the news reports.

Say exactly why you are writing.

I'm writing with a request. Can you please play 'Heart Attack' by Natalie Barrett for my boyfriend, Mark, next Saturday because it's his birthday? Thank you.

Close your letter and write your name.

With best wishes,
Caroline Taggart

Project ① *Snapshot of where I live*

Write a project about the place where you live, your home and family, and your life there. Use photographs and pictures from magazines to illustrate your project.

Where do you live?
What sort of place is it?
What's it famous for?

My name's Katie Brennan. I live in Liverpool, a big city in the north-west of England. It's a great place to live. Liverpool is famous for The Beatles and it's got two great football teams, Liverpool and Everton. There are some big shops, lots of clubs and discos and there are also some interesting museums and art galleries.

What's your home like?
Who do you live with?

I live in a flat. It's on the top floor of a student hostel. I'm lucky because my bedroom's quite big and I've got a great view. I live with my mother, father and brother Sam. My mother is the hostel warden and my father's a lecturer at Liverpool University.

Write about your typical Saturday.
What do you do? Where do you go?

On Saturday I usually get up late and watch TV. In the afternoon I often meet my friends in town. We sometimes go to the cinema and then have a pizza, or we just hang around the shopping centre. In the winter I sometimes go ten-pin bowling with my friends or go to a football match with Sam and my Dad.

Everybody's talking from the film *Midnight Cowboy* was a hit for the American singer Harry Nilsson in 1969. It is now a classic pop song.

Everybody's talking

Everybody's talking at me
I don't hear a word [1]............ ,
Only the echoes of my mind.
People [2]............ and stare.
[3] .... their faces,
Only the shadows of their eyes.

[4] .... where the sun keeps shining
Through the [5]............ ,
Going where the weather suits my clothes,
Backing off of the north-east wind
[6]............ on a summer breeze,
Skipping over the ocean like a stone*.
Ohooo

.... where the sun keeps shining
Through the .... ,
Going where the weather suits my clothes,
Backing off of the north-east wind
.... on a summer breeze,
Skipping over the ocean like a stone*.

Everybody's talking at me.
I can't hear a word .... ,
Only the echoes of my mind.
I won't let you leave my love behind
I won't let you leave, oh, oh
Won't let you leave my love behind.

* When you throw a flat stone on to water it 'skips'
or *bounces* over the surface a few times.

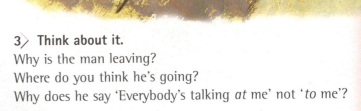

1> (••) Read the lyrics of the song and guess
which of these words or phrases fits each gap.
Then listen and see if you were right.
• pouring rain   • I'm going   • sailing
• they're saying   • I can't see   • stop

2> Guess the meaning of these words from the
song.
• echoes   • to stare   • shadows   • to suit
• breeze

3> **Think about it.**
Why is the man leaving?
Where do you think he's going?
Why does he say 'Everybody's talking *at* me' not '*to* me'?

6 > Who are they playing?

Learning goals

Communication
Make polite requests with *could*

Grammar
Present continuous as future
Gerund (*-ing* form) after verbs
  like, hate, (don't) mind, prefer
Defining relative clauses with
  who, which, where

Vocabulary
Months and dates
Sports/Sports locations

Before you listen

Do you ever go to football matches?
Who do you go with?
Are the tickets expensive?
Who's your favourite team?

1 > 👀 Listen and read

Joe: Excuse me, could we look at your *What's on?* magazine, please?

Girl: Sure. Go ahead.

Joe: Thanks. Look! Liverpool are playing at Anfield tomorrow night.

Gabriel: Who are they playing?

Joe: Barcelona. It's a friendly match.

Gabriel: Barcelona! I'd really like to see that!

Stefan: Me too.

Joe: Mick, could you get us some tickets for tomorrow's match?

Mick: I'm sorry, I can't. It's too late. But there are sometimes some tickets at the gate, if you don't mind queuing.

Gabriel: I don't mind queuing to see Barcelona. Do you want to come, Sandra?

Sandra: No, thanks. I'm not very keen on football. I prefer swimming.

Spike: Yuk! I hate swimming. I hate putting my head under water!

> **LIVERPOOL FC** V **BARCELONA**
> **AT: ANFIELD**
> **DATE: 12TH AUGUST**
> **KICK OFF: 7.30 P.M.**

2 > Comprehension

a> Answer the questions.

1 Which two teams are playing at Anfield?
2 What must the group do to get a ticket?
3 Which sport does Sandra prefer?

b> Who wants to go to the match?
Answer Y (yes), N (no) or DK (don't know).

• Joe? • Spike? • Gabriel? • Sandra?
• Stefan? • Louise?

Grammar snapshot

Present continuous as future

We're **going** to a football match tonight.
Liverpool **are playing** Barcelona tomorrow.

Compare.

Do you have more than one way of talking about the future in your language?

 Useful phrases

3>

Listen and repeat.

- Sure.
- Go ahead.
- Look!
- Me too.

- I'm sorry, I can't.
- I'm not very keen on [football].
- Yuk!

4> **Memory bank**

Months and dates

What are these dates in words?

1 1st Aug 1965 = *the first of August nineteen sixty-five*

2 2nd Sept 1974 =

3 3rd Nov 1980 =

4 14th Oct 1997 =

Complete these phrases with the correct prepositions.

5 ... August

6 ... 1965

7 ... 1st August 1965

Some important future sporting events for your diary

Brazilian Football (Copa do Brasil)

Teams:	**Flamengo v. Palmeiras**
Date:	**21st August**
Place:	**Parque Antárctica, São Paulo**

Exhibition Tennis Match

Players:	**Sampras v. Ivanisevic**
Date:	**3rd September**
Place:	**Zagreb**

Basketball Major League

Teams:	**Harlem Globetrotters v. Boston Allstars**
Date:	**22nd November**
Place:	**Madison Square Garden, New York**

5> **Practice**

Look at the list of sporting events. Use the prompts below and the present continuous tense to talk about them.

A: *Who are Flamengo playing next?*
B: *They're playing Palmeiras.*

- Who/play/next?
- When/play?
- Where/match/take place?

WATER BABY or FOOTBALL FREAK?

What's your rating? Mark the boxes: ✓ = Yes   ✗ = No

Do you like:

1 (swim) under water? ☐
2 (dive) off the top board? ☐
3 (swim) in the sea? ☐

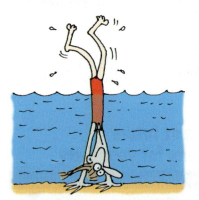

Do you mind:

4 (put) your head under water? ☐
5 (get) water in your eyes? ☐

Do you prefer:

6a) (have) fun in the water? ☐
 b) (swim) lots of lengths? ☐
7a) (do) the crawl? ☐
 b) (do) breaststroke? ☐
8a) (jump) straight into the water? ☐
 b) (walk) in slowly? ☐

Do you like:

 9 (sing and shout) at matches? ☐
10 (go) to live matches? ☐
11 (buy) football strips and souvenirs? ☐

Do you mind:

12 (sit) with the other team's supporters? ☐
13 (queue) for tickets for football matches? ☐

Do you prefer:

14a) (stand) near the goal? ☐
 b) (sit) at the side of the pitch? ☐
15a) (play) football? ☐
 b) (watch) it? ☐
16a) (wear) your team's colours? ☐
 b) (wear) your own clothes? ☐

Your rating

Water baby			Football freak		
1	Yes **1**	No **0**	9	Yes **1**	No **0**
2	Yes **1**	No **0**	10	Yes **1**	No **0**
3	Yes **1**	No **0**	11	Yes **1**	No **0**
4	Yes **0**	No **1**	12	Yes **0**	No **1**
5	Yes **0**	No **1**	13	Yes **0**	No **1**
6	a) **0**	b) **1**	14	a) **1**	b) **0**
7	a) **1**	b) **0**	15	a) **1**	b) **0**
8	a) **1**	b) **0**	16	a) **1**	b) **0**

Water baby rating

6–8: You are a real water baby. You love water and everything about it. Is your star sign Pisces by any chance?

3–5: You like swimming but you are not crazy about it. Are you 'middle-of-the-road' about everything?

Below 3: You hate going in the water. Do you hate having a bath too?

Football freak rating

6–8: You are a real football freak. Is football the only thing in your life?

3–5: You like watching or playing football but you also like doing other things as well. Are you so perfect?

Below 3: You don't really like football, do you? What's wrong with it?

Grammar snapshot

Gerund (-*ing* form) after verbs *like*, *hate*,
(don't) mind, *prefer*
I like div**ing**.
I hate swim**ming**.
I don't mind queu**ing**. (= It's OK.)
I prefer swim**ming** to run**ning**.

Make rules.
When we use the *-ing* form what happens to:
1 the spelling of verbs like *swim*, *run*, *put* and *get*?
2 the spelling of verbs like *dive*, *take* and *have*?

6> Practice

a> Complete the questionnaire using the verb (in brackets). Then ask and answer the questions with a partner to find your partner's rating.

A: *Do you like diving off the top board?*
B: *Yes, I do. / No, I don't.*
A: *Do you mind putting your head under water?*
B: *Yes, I do. I hate it. / No, I don't mind. It's OK.*

b> Tell the class about your partner's answers.

Gianfranco likes swimming in the sea but he doesn't like diving or swimming under water. He prefers swimming breaststroke to doing the crawl. His 'water baby rating' is 3.

7> Vocabulary

Sports and sports locations

Look at the symbols and name each sport. Then match the sport with a word which describes where it takes place.

1 tennis court

• course • pitch • court • pool • track • circuit

8> ⸛ Listen

Listen to the radio programme about four future sporting events and copy and complete the chart.

Sport	Venue	Date
1	Silverstone	
2	The Millennium Sports Centre	
3	Royal Albert Hall	
4	Crystal Palace National Sports Centre	

9> Over to you

Talk about sport.
1 What's your favourite sport?
2 When's the next big match and where is it?
3 Who's playing/competing?

10> ⸛ Sound**bite**   The sound / θ /

third   eigh**th**   nin**th**
(Look at page 122.)

11> Communication

Making polite requests with *could*

▶ Could we look at your *What's on?* magazine, please?
▷ Sure. Go ahead. / Certainly. / I'm sorry. I'm afraid
   I need it.
▶ Could you get us some tickets, please?
▷ Yes. OK. / I'm sorry. I'm afraid I can't.

Make requests for the following situations.

1 You want your teacher to check your work.
2 You want a friend to video *The Big Match* for
   you this evening.
3 You want a friend to lend you his/her CD player.
4 You and a friend want to use the school
   computer after school. Ask your teacher.

Young, talented and good-looking

Jamie Redknapp, who started his football career with Liverpool FC, is one of England's most famous footballers.

1 _____?

No, I don't. Football's my life. Even in my spare time I like watching videos of other matches.

2 _____?

Yes, I do. They usually just ask for signed photos, but I sometimes get letters which are quite embarrassing. They ask for bits of my hair and clothes!

3 _____?

No, I don't. At the moment I'm lodging with a family near the ground where we train.

4 _____?

I enjoy going out, meeting friends – you know, the usual things. At the moment, I'm also doing some modelling, so I don't really have a lot of free time.

5 _____?

That's my secret. I'm not telling, I'm afraid!

6 _____?

Well, I'm often late for interviews with newspaper reporters and sometimes I don't turn up at all. You're lucky!

7 _____?

I don't know what I'm going to do when I'm too old to play football. I don't want to be a coach. My Dad's a football coach and I know it's a hard job.

12 ▷ Read

Read the interview with Jamie Redknapp and put the questions in the correct places.

a) How much do you earn a week?
b) Is there life after football for you?
c) I suppose you live in a fabulous flat?
d) Have you got any bad qualities?
e) What do you like doing in your free time?
f) Do you ever get bored with football?
g) Do you get a lot of letters from female fans?

Grammar flash

Defining relative clauses with *who, which, where*
Jamie Redknapp is a Liverpool footballer **who** is always in the news.
I sometimes get letters **which** are quite embarrassing.
It's near the ground **where** we train.

Make a rule.
We use ... to refer to people, ... to refer to places and ... to refer to things.

13 ▷ Practice

Complete the sentences with *who, which* **or** *where*.

1 Anfield is the name of the stadium ... Liverpool FC play.
2 The team ... scores the most goals wins the Cup.
3 The coach is the person ... trains the players.
4 The shop next to the stadium is one of the places ... you can buy photographs of the famous players.
5 The 'player of the season' is usually the one ... scores most goals.
6 The competition ... attracts most people is the World Cup.

14 ▷ Write

Write an interview for a magazine.

Imagine you are a sports journalist. Write a short interview with your favourite sports star.

An afternoon in town

Read the story and put the pictures in the correct order. Then listen and see if you were right.

1 = Picture D

Yuk! I hate strawberry.

What flavour would you like?

Could I have chocolate, please?

A

What about you, Louise? Do you want to come?

No, thanks. I'm going back to the hostel.

B

Look! There's an ice cream van.

Brilliant!

C

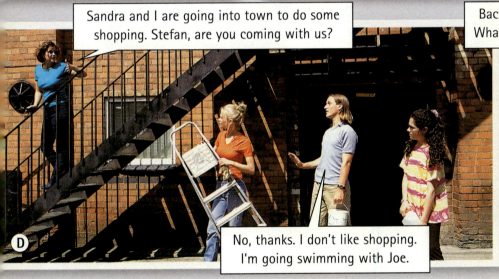

Sandra and I are going into town to do some shopping. Stefan, are you coming with us?

No, thanks. I don't like shopping. I'm going swimming with Joe.

D

Back to the hostel? What? On your own?

It's OK. I don't mind being on my own.

OK. See you later.

E

Come on, Spike. We mustn't be late for supper!

Take it easy, Sandra. Just enjoy your ice cream. I hate rushing!

F

Can I help you?

Yes. Could I have a strawberry cone, please?

Yes, certainly.

G

41

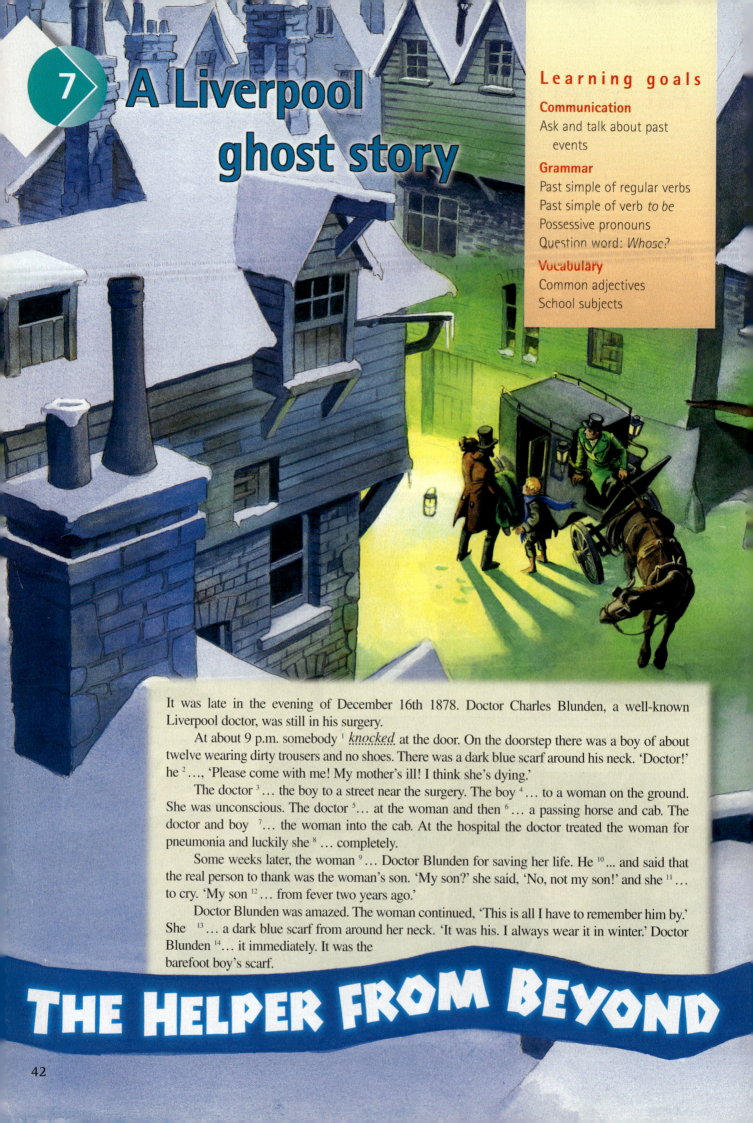

7 A Liverpool ghost story

Learning goals

Communication
Ask and talk about past events

Grammar
Past simple of regular verbs
Past simple of verb *to be*
Possessive pronouns
Question word: *Whose?*

Vocabulary
Common adjectives
School subjects

It was late in the evening of December 16th 1878. Doctor Charles Blunden, a well-known Liverpool doctor, was still in his surgery.

At about 9 p.m. somebody ¹ *knocked* at the door. On the doorstep there was a boy of about twelve wearing dirty trousers and no shoes. There was a dark blue scarf around his neck. 'Doctor!' he ² ..., 'Please come with me! My mother's ill! I think she's dying.'

The doctor ³ ... the boy to a street near the surgery. The boy ⁴ ... to a woman on the ground. She was unconscious. The doctor ⁵ ... at the woman and then ⁶ ... a passing horse and cab. The doctor and boy ⁷ ... the woman into the cab. At the hospital the doctor treated the woman for pneumonia and luckily she ⁸ ... completely.

Some weeks later, the woman ⁹ ... Doctor Blunden for saving her life. He ¹⁰ ... and said that the real person to thank was the woman's son. 'My son?' she said, 'No, not my son!' and she ¹¹ ... to cry. 'My son ¹² ... from fever two years ago.'

Doctor Blunden was amazed. The woman continued, 'This is all I have to remember him by.' She ¹³ ... a dark blue scarf from around her neck. 'It was his. I always wear it in winter.' Doctor Blunden ¹⁴ ... it immediately. It was the barefoot boy's scarf.

THE HELPER FROM BEYOND

1  Read and listen

Complete the story with these past tense verbs. Then listen and see if you were right.

• pointed • pulled • smiled • knocked • stopped
• recognised • looked • cried • died • recovered
• started • followed • lifted • thanked

Grammar snapshot

Past simple of regular verbs

Infinitive	Past simple
start	started
smile	smiled

Positive statements	Negative statements
A boy knocked at the door.	He ... enter the house.

Questions	Short answers
	Positive Negative
... the woman recover?	Yes, she ... . No, she ... .

What are the missing words?

Note these spelling changes.

stop	stop**ped**
cry	cri**ed**

2  Soundbite The sounds / t /, / d / and / ɪd /

stop**ped**   listen**ed**   want**ed**
(Look at page 122.)

3 Practice

Put the verbs in brackets into the past simple tense to complete the sentences. Then write the events in the order in which they happened. Sentences a) and h) are in the correct order.

1 a) *One evening, a boy wearing a blue scarf knocked at the door of Dr Blunden's surgery.*

b) The woman (thank) the doctor.

c) The boy and the doctor (walk) to a nearby street.

d) The boy (point) to his mother, who was unconscious in the snow.

e) The doctor (explain) that the person to thank was the woman's son.

f) The boy (ask) the doctor to help his mother.

g) The doctor (treat) the woman in hospital and (save) her life.

8 h) *The woman said her son had died two years ago and showed the doctor the boy's blue scarf.*

THE GRAVE

4 Listen and read

Stefan: I finished your book of ghost stories, Joe. It was really good.
Spike: Ghost stories! They're a load of rubbish!
Joe: You're not in a very good mood, Spike. What's up?
Spike: I'm expecting my exam results today. Have you got yours?
Joe: Yes. Mine arrived yesterday.
Spike: How were they?
Joe: They weren't bad. In fact, I did quite well.
Spike: I'm really worried about mine.

5 Comprehension

Answer the questions.

1 Why is Spike in a bad mood?
2 What were Joe's results like?
3 How does Spike feel about her results?
4 When did Spike's father phone?

Later
Stella: Oh, Spike. Your father phoned at lunchtime.
Spike: Did he leave a message?
Stella: No, he didn't.
Spike: I bet it was about my exam results.
Joe: Go and phone him and find out.
Spike: No! I don't want to know!
Joe: Go on, Spike. Do it!

6 🔊 Useful phrases

Listen and repeat.

- [They're] a load of rubbish.
- [You're not] in a very good mood.
- What's up?
- I'm really worried about [my results].
- Go on!
- Do it!

7 Memory bank

Common adjectives

- big • easy • expensive • new
- boring • late • heavy • awful
- slow • strong • old • tall

Which are the opposite adjectives? Write the pairs in your vocabulary notebook.

1 big – small

Grammar flash

Past simple of verb *to be*	
I **was/wasn't**	at school today.
They **were/weren't**	

was *(I, he, she, it)*
were *(you, we, they)*

8 Communication

Asking and talking about past events

exams?/fine/Maths exam/difficult?/
quite easy

▶ How were your exams?/What were your exams like?
▶ They were fine.
▶ Was the Maths exam difficult?
▶ No, it wasn't. It was quite easy.

Make conversations with these prompts.

1 Oasis concert?/brilliant/difficult to get tickets?/easy
2 holiday?/OK/weather good?/awful
3 English exam?/all right/questions easy?/quite difficult
4 film?/long/very good?/a load of rubbish

9 Over to you

Ask the questions below. If the answer is 'Yes', ask another question to find out more details.

Last weekend did you ...

- phone a friend? (Who? How long/talk for?)
- visit a website on the Internet? (Which?)
- watch television? (Which programme? What was it like?)
- listen to some new albums? (What?)
- play a computer game? (Which? What was your score?)
- play a game or sport? (What? Where?)
- travel by bus or train? (Where to?)

Now tell the class about your partner.

Grammar flash

Possessive pronouns

Singular		Plural	
my	→ **mine**	our	→ **ours**
your	→ **yours**	your	→ **yours**
her	→ **hers**	their	→ **theirs**
his	→ **his**		

Question word: *Whose?*
Whose bag is this? It's mine.

10 Practice

Complete the sentences with the correct possessive pronouns.

1 A: Sandra, is this your bag?
   B: No, that's ... over there.
2 A: Which is Spike's room?
   B: ... is number five.
3 A: Is that Tina and Jeff's flat?
   B: No, it isn't. ... hasn't got a balcony.
4 A: These are not my books.
   B: That's right. ... are in the cupboard.
5 A: Is this Stefan's guitar?
   B: No, ... is a Spanish guitar.

- English Language
- English Literature
- Maths
- Science
- Modern languages: French, German or Spanish
- Geography
- History
- Design and Technology
- Computer studies
- Environmental studies
- Physical Education
- Music
- Art
- Religious studies
- Media studies

11 > Vocabulary

School subjects

Read the list of subjects.

1 Which subjects are the students studying in the pictures?
2 Which of these subjects do you study?
3 What other subjects are on your timetable?

12 > •• Listen

a> Spike phones her father to find out about her exam results. Listen and note her grades for:

English Language	☐	Biology	☐
English Literature	☐	History	☐
Maths	☐	Art	☐
French	☐		

b> **Answer the questions.**

1 Is Spike pleased with her exam results?
2 Why is she upset about her grade in Art?
3 What does Spike want to do?
4 What two suggestions does her father make?
5 What are Spike and her parents going to do when Spike gets home?

13 > Helpline

Record past tense forms of regular verbs.

It is a good idea to note down verbs with their infinitive and past tense forms.

Infinitive	Past tense
point	pointed
stop	stopped
cry	cried

List the verbs in this unit in the infinitive and past tense.

Fast rewind UNITS 6 and 7

Grammar

1⟩ Use the present continuous of the verbs in brackets to make sentences about the future.

(you/play) ... in the match on Saturday?
Are you playing in the match on Saturday?

1 (My brother/take) ... his guitar exam in June.
2 (She/not go) ... to England this summer.
3 (they/come) ... to your birthday party?
4 (We/travel) ... by train, not by car.
5 (I/leave) ... on Thursday next week.

2⟩ Complete the text with the verbs in brackets in the past simple tense.

'Helen's birthday party (be) [1] *was* very good. I really (enjoy) [2] ... it. There (be) [3] ... about fifty people there. I (talk) [4] ... to a boy called Mick and we (dance) [5] ... most of the evening. At midnight everyone (play) [6] ... silly games but we just (listen) [7] ... to music. I (miss) [8] ... the last bus so Mick (walk) [9] ... home with me. He's really nice.'

3⟩ Complete the short answers.

Did Kate go out with Sam? Yes, *she did.*

1 Were you angry with me? Yes, ...
2 Did you go to the cinema last night? No, ...
3 Was the film good? Yes, ...
4 Were the shops open? No, ...
5 Did your parents give you any money? Yes, ...
6 Was Mark wearing his leather jacket? No, ...

4⟩ Use a verb in the -ing form to make sentences.

• do • listen to • take • dance • swim • have • get up

My father loves *taking* the dog for a walk every evening.

1 In summer we love ... in the lake.
2 She hates ... early.
3 I don't like ... cold showers.
4 The students all love ... history projects.
5 My parents don't enjoy ... my CDs.
6 My sister goes to discos a lot because she loves ... .

5⟩ Complete the sentences with *which, where* or *who*.

That's the house *where* I was born.

1 Do you know the people ... live in the flat next to you?
2 I know a story ... is going to make you laugh.
3 Do you know a place ... I can learn to scuba-dive?
4 Don't take anything ... isn't yours.
5 I've got a friend ... goes to school in Paris.
6 In Italy there are a lot of restaurants ... children are welcome.

6⟩ Complete the sentences with the correct possessive pronoun.

• ours • theirs • mine • yours • his • hers

You've got your own ruler. Don't take *mine*.

1 I haven't got a pen. Can I borrow ..., Joe?
2 This isn't Spike's room. ... is always untidy!
3 That's not Stella and David's car. ... is a Fiat.
4 Have your sandwiches now. We're going to have ... later.
5 No, it isn't Stefan's guitar. He keeps ... in his room.

Vocabulary

7⟩ Sort the words into four groups: months of the year, sports locations, school subjects and adjectives.

• heavy • Science • November • track • Geography
• cheap • pool • July • pitch • May • Maths • court
• February • boring • History • early • March • old
• Physics • circuit

Communication

8⟩ Work in pairs. Student A:
Ask Student B
• what subjects he/she hates doing at school.
• when his/her birthday is.
• what he/she is doing this evening.
• what he/she did last weekend.

Now Student B:
Ask Student A
• what things he/she likes doing on Sunday.
• what date it is tomorrow.
• what his/her plans are for Saturday evening.
• what he/she watched on TV last night.

Progress update Units 6 and 7

How do you rate your progress? Tick the chart.

	Excellent ★★★★	Good ★★★	OK ★★	Can do better ★
Grammar				
Vocabulary				
Communication				

8 ▷ Girls screamed and wept.

Learning goals

Communication
Give biographical details
Buy things in shops
Ask for and give directions

Grammar
Past simple of irregular verbs

Vocabulary
English money
Places in towns

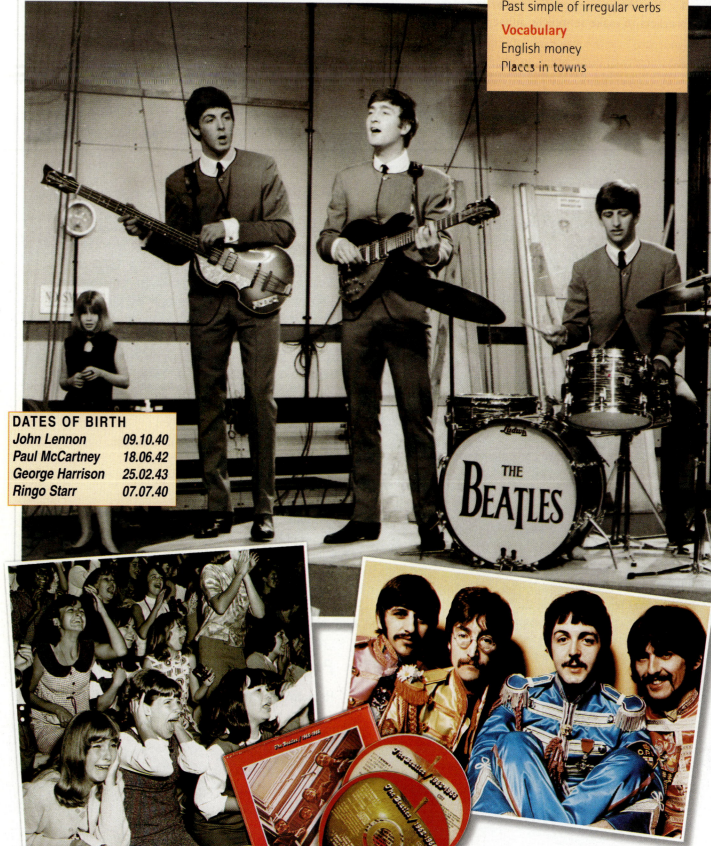

DATES OF BIRTH

John Lennon	09.10.40
Paul McCartney	18.06.42
George Harrison	25.02.43
Ringo Starr	07.07.40

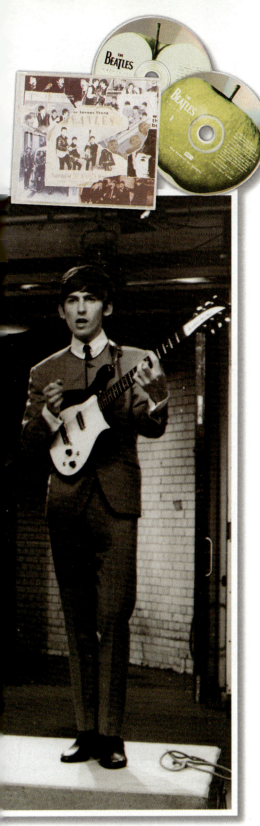

Before you read

What do you know about The Beatles?

Have you got any Beatles CDs or cassettes at home?

Do you like their music?

What sort of music do you like?

Do you or any of your friends play or sing with a band?

1> Read

The four Beatles – John Lennon, Paul McCartney, George Harrison and Ringo Starr – were all born in Liverpool. John, Paul and George knew each other at school and played together in a guitar-based rock band called The Quarrymen in 1959. They were in their late teens. Ringo Starr didn't join the group until 1962, after Stuart Sutcliffe, 'the fifth Beatle', died. John, George and Paul played rhythm, lead and bass guitars. Ringo played the drums.

The Beatles started their career at the Cavern Club in Liverpool. They first appeared there without Ringo on 21st February 1961. On 9th November Brian Epstein, a local record shop owner, saw The Beatles at a lunchtime session. He met them and a month later he became their manager. Brian Epstein gave The Beatles a new image – the famous Beatles suits and Beatles haircut.

In 1963 the group had their first Number 1 hit record in the UK charts with their single, *Please Please Me*. They gave their first US concert on 11th February 1964. By April 1964 The Beatles were top of the UK singles and album charts and they held the top five places in the US charts.

The next two years were the high point of Beatlemania. Girls screamed and wept when they went to Beatles' concerts. Everybody bought their records. By 1966 The Beatles had eight more Number 1 hit singles and five Number 1 albums.

In 1967 The Beatles made their most creative album, *Sergeant Pepper's Lonely Hearts Club Band*. In the same year they went to India and became followers of the Maharishi Mahesh Yogi. From then on, nothing was ever quite the same. Gradually, Beatlemania faded and, in 1968, the four Beatles started to go their different ways. In 1971 they finally split up.

But the music of The Beatles didn't die. It had something special, and their music is still very popular today.

2> Comprehension

Read the text again and write a date for each headline. Then put the headlines in correct chronological order

A 1967

(A) *Sergeant Pepper* – best ever Beatles album?

(B) **Fab Four top of US charts**

(C) **Beatles break up**

(D) **New group sensation at Cavern Club**

(E) **Beatles go to India**

(F) **Liverpool group have first No. 1 hit**

(G) **New Beatles drummer**

Grammar snapshot

Past simple of irregular verbs

Positive statements
He saw them in Liverpool.

Negative statements
He ... them in London.

Questions

Did he ... them in London?
Where did he see them?

Short answers

Positive
Yes, he ... .

Negative
No, he ... .

What are the missing words?

Compare.
Are there any irregular past tense forms in your language?

3〉 Practice

a〉 Give the past tense forms of these verbs. Then look back at the text about The Beatles to check your answers.

become *became*

- become • buy • have • hold • give • go
- know • make • meet • see • weep

b〉 Complete the dialogue with the correct form of the verbs.

A: What (do) [1] *did* you *do* at the weekend?
B: On Saturday 1 (go) [2] ... to an exhibition about The Beatles with my friend. And we (buy) [3] ... some things from the souvenir shop.
A: What (buy) [4] ... you ...?
B: Some postcards and a CD. What (do) [5] ... you ... last weekend?
A: 1 (not do) [6] ... anything special. 1 (go) [7] ... to the cinema with my brother.
B: What (see) [8] ... you ... ?
A: We (see) [9] ... *Batman V.* Oh, and we (meet) [10] ... Julia outside the cinema. Then we (have) [11] ... a hamburger.

4〉 **Help**line

↓

Learn past tense forms of irregular verbs.

Make a list of verbs which have irregular past tenses. Note that some verbs are the same in the infinitive and past tense.

Infinitive	Past tense
make	made
put	put
write	wrote

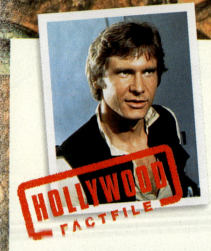

He's Han Solo and Indiana Jones. He's the star of many Hollywood blockbusters. His name is **Harrison Ford**.

Born: ......
Parents: Christopher and Dorothy
First hobby: ......
Aged 12: Becomes a student at Meltzer Junior High School (1954–60)
Aged 18: ......
Outside college: Forms a band, The Brothers Gross, with a friend
Aged 22: ......
Aged 24: Gets first part in film in 1966
Aged 30: ......
Job: Works as a carpenter and makes furniture in Hollywood
Aged 34: ......
Some other important films: *The Empire Strikes Back, Raiders of the Lost Ark, Blade Runner, Witness, Working Girl, The Fugitive, The Devil's Own, Air Force One*

5〉 Interaction

Student B: Turn to page 121 and follow the instructions.
Student A: Ask Student B questions to complete your factfile on Harrison Ford. Then answer Student B's questions.

A: *When and where was Harrison Ford born?*
B: *He was born on ... in ...*
A: *What was his first hobby?*
B: *He ...*
A: *What happened/did he do when he was 18?*
B: *He ...*

6 Memory bank   English money

Notes: £50, £20, £10, £5
Coins: £1, 50p, 20p, 10p, 5p, 2p, 1p
p = pence/p
£1= a pound (100 pence)
£1.50 = one pound fifty (pence)
£3.45 = three pounds forty-five (pence)

7 Listen

a Listen to Louise, Spike and Gabriel in the souvenir shop at 'The Beatles Story' exhibition. Note down:

1 why they went into the souvenir shop.
2 what they bought.
3 how much it cost.
4 what value note Louise gave the assistant.
5 what the assistant gave them as a free gift.

b In pairs, check your answers like this:

A: *Why did they go into the souvenir shop?*
B: *Because Louise wanted to ...*

8 Communication

Buying things in shops

▶ Excuse me, how much is this Oasis CD?
▶ It's £9.99.
▶ OK. I'll have it. Have you got change for a £20 note?
▶ Yes, certainly. Here you are. Ten pounds and a penny.

You are shopping in town. Take turns with your partner to buy these things.

1 a Queen calendar – £2.50 (you have a £5 note)
2 a Madonna T-shirt – £7.99 (you have a £10 note)
3 a Kula Shaker CD – £13. 99 (you have a £20 note)
4 a black denim jacket – £39.50 (you have a £50 note)

51

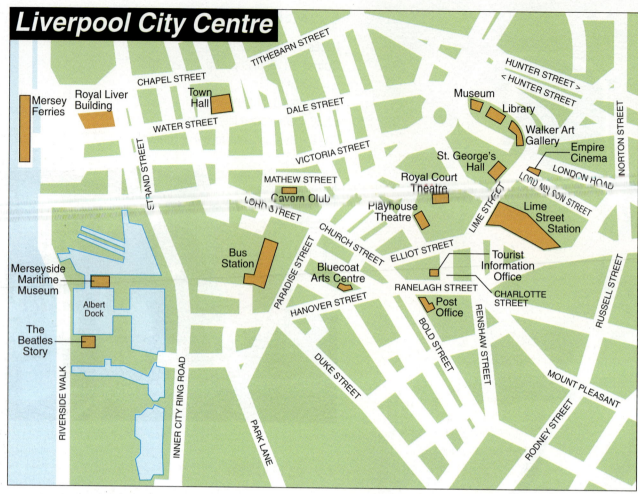

Liverpool City Centre

9 > Communication

Asking for and giving directions

▶ Excuse me, can you tell me the way to ... ?

▶ Yes, sure/certainly. | Go down this street.
Go straight ahead.
Turn left/right (into ... Street).
Take the first turning on the left.
Take the second turning on the right.

▶ Is it far?

▶ No, you can walk there in five minutes.
The ... is | on the left.
on the right.
in front of you.
on the corner of ... .

▶ Thanks very much.

You are outside the Tourist Information Office in Charlotte Street. Use the map of the centre of Liverpool to ask for and give directions to:

1 Lime Street Station   3 the Playhouse Theatre
2 the Empire Cinema   4 the Cavern Club

10 > Listen

Listen to the dialogues and see if you were right.

11 > Memory bank

Places in towns

Which places can you find on the map of Liverpool? Make a list.

railway station, library, ...

Add any other places you can think of:

ice rink, ...

12 > Over to you

Write down the names of three places near your school that you can walk to:

• in two minutes   • in five minutes
• in ten minutes

Do not show your partner your list. Give directions to the places, and see if your partner can guess what they are.

At the Cavern Club

🔊 **Read the story and put the pictures in the correct order. Then listen and see if you were right.**

1 = Picture C

A

Where exactly is the Cavern Club?

We're nearly there. We take the next turning on the left.

Who's making all that noise down there?

Sssh! It's Stella! We woke her up!

Next time, don't forget your keys!

B

C

Sandra, do you want to come to the Cavern Club tonight?

Yes, sure.

What about Stefan? Does he want to come? Where is he?

I don't know. I think he went to the cinema with Joe.

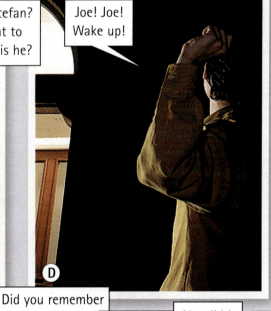

D

Joe! Joe! Wake up!

E

Louise! Come on! You're the one who can dance!

It's OK. I prefer to watch.

I'm sure there's something wrong with Louise.

F

How much is a packet of sugar-free gum?

Thirty-five pence.

OK. I'll have two packets, please.

G

Did you remember to bring a key? I didn't.

No, I didn't.

Nor did I.

I think we've got a bit of a problem.

H

Just a minute. I must get some gum before we go into the club.

CAVERN NEWSAGENTS

9 ▷ What was it doing?

Learning goals

Communication
Describe past events

Grammar
Past continuous
Time clauses with *when/ while*

Vocabulary
Animals
Rooms and parts of the house

1▷ Vocabulary Animals

Name the animals in the pictures. Choose from the following.

Number 1 is a parrot.

- cow • fox • dog • giraffe • pig • cat
- kangaroo • lion • horse • sheep • duck
- goat • tiger • rabbit • chicken • snake
- lamb • rhinoceros • budgie • elephant
- parrot • koala bear • goldfish
- crocodile • spider

2 Practice

Look at the people below. Which animal would each person like as a pet? Give your reasons. Then turn to page 121 and check.

I think Mrs Williams would like ...

Mrs Monica Williams lives in London She is 72.

Sue Allan lives in a student hostel. She is 19.

Stephen Fairley lives on a farm in Scotland. He is 7.

3 Over to you

Answer the questions.

Have you got any animals at home?
Which animal would you like to have as a pet?

4 ⟨••⟩ Soundbite

The sounds / ɔː / and / ɒ /

ho**rse** f**o**x   (Look at page 122.)

5 ⟨••⟩ Listen and read

Katie: Something smells good! What's going on?
Gabriel: We're making Joe's birthday cake.
Sandra: It's a surprise.
Sam: Guess what! We saw a parrot on the way home!
Sandra: A parrot! Where?
Sam: We saw it when we were walking back from the cinema.
Sandra: What was it doing?
Katie: Nothing much. It was just flying across the road.
Gabriel: That's strange! Parrots can't live in the wild in Britain.
          It's too cold.
Sam: Perhaps it was somebody's pet and it escaped.
          Hey! Can I have a taste of that?
Sandra: No, hands off!

6 Comprehension

Answer T (true), F (false) or DK (don't know).

1 Gabriel and Sandra are making a cake.
2 Joe knows about the cake.
3 Katie and Sam saw a parrot outside the house.
4 They were on their bicycles.
5 The parrot saw them.
6 There are lots of wild parrots in Britain.
7 Sandra lets Sam taste the cake.

7 ⟨••⟩ Useful phrases

Listen and repeat.

• Something smells good!
• It's a surprise.
• Guess what!
• Nothing much.
• That's strange!
• Hands off!

Grammar snapshot

Past continuous

Positive statements		Negative statements	
I was	walking.	I wasn't	running.
You were		You weren't	
She was		She wasn't	

Questions		Short answers	
		Positive	Negative
Was I	walking?	Yes, you were.	No, you weren't.
Were you		Yes, I was.	No, I wasn't.
Was she		Yes, she was.	No, she wasn't.

Make a similar table with statements, questions and short answers using the pronouns *he*, *it*, *we* and *they*.

Time clauses with *when* / *while*

While Katie and Sam were walking back from the cinema they saw a parrot.

Katie and Sam were walking back from the cinema **when** they saw a parrot.

What were Katie and Sam doing **when** they saw the parrot?

8 > Memory bank

Rooms and parts of the house

- library • pool • kitchen • bathroom • toilet
- dining room • sitting room • hall • bedroom
- study • balcony • garage • patio • garden

9 > Practice

A group of film stars were spending the weekend in a Hollywood mansion. At 7p.m. on Saturday they heard a scream in the garden.

a > Say where the film stars were at 7p.m.

1 Bruce Willis and Mel Gibson were in the library.

b > Take turns to ask and answer about the film stars. Follow the cues and use the past continuous tense.

A: *What were Bruce Willis and Mel Gibson doing?*
B: *They were playing cards.*

1 What / Bruce Willis and Mel Gibson / do?
2 Who / Brad Pitt / sit / next to?
3 Where / Sandra Bullock / wash / her hair?
4 What / Madonna / make?
5 Where / Kate Winslet / swim?
6 Who / Nicole Kidman / have / supper with?

10 > Over to you

What were you doing at these times?

1 Yesterday at:

a.m.	7.30	8.15	10.00
p.m.	1.30	7.00	10.00

2 Last Saturday at:

a.m.	9.00	11.00
p.m.	3.00	4.00

At half past seven yesterday morning I was watching The Breakfast Show on TV.

At three o'clock last Saturday afternoon I ...

1 Bruce Willis / Mel Gibson

4 Madonna

11 〉 Communication

Describing past events

▶ There was a robbery in my street this morning.
▶ Did you see anything?
▶ Yes, I saw two men.
▶ What were they doing?
▶ They were running out of the bank.

Use the conversation and your imagination to talk about an incident (e.g. a robbery, an accident or a mugging) in one of the following places.

- at a supermarket
- in a games arcade
- at a football match
- in the street

12 〉 👓 Listen

It's Joe's birthday party. Listen to the dialogue and put these events in the correct order.

a) He blew out the candles on the cake.
b) He opened his present.
c) They played a Beatles album.
d) They all said 'Happy Birthday, Joe'.
e) He thanked them for the cake.

13 〉 **Help**line

Use a dictionary (1).

1 Read the whole text for general meaning.
2 Only look up words and expressions if you can't guess their meaning.
3 Go through all the meanings in the dictionary until you find the right one.
4 With expressions containing several words, look up the main word first.

Now turn to page 58 and try your dictionary skills.

2 Brad Pitt / Julia Roberts

3 Sandra Bullock

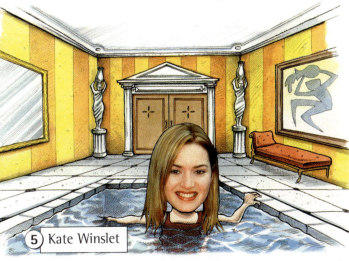

5 Kate Winslet

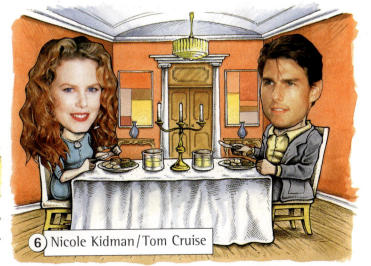

6 Nicole Kidman / Tom Cruise

True life   True life   True Li

A lucky escape

Stig was a big Alsatian dog who was becoming a bit of a problem. He lived with the Svensson family in their eighth-floor flat in Malmo in Sweden, but he was growing too big for the flat. The Svenssons were also worried that Stig was a danger to their two-year-old daughter, Mariette.

Then one day something extraordinary happened. Leif Svensson walked into the bedroom and noticed that the window was open. To his horror he saw that Mariette was crawling along the narrow ledge outside and Stig the Alsatian was following her along the ledge, only centimetres away.

Leif shouted for his wife. When she arrived, Stig was next to Mariette. Leif and his wife were beginning to fear the worst when suddenly the dog took the little girl's trousers in his teeth and started to walk slowly backwards along the ledge. Stig carried the child back to the open window and Leif pulled them both inside.

'We can never repay Stig,' said Leif later. 'He saved Mariette's life. From now on we're going to feed him the best steak that money can buy!'

Before you read

Why do you think people keep dogs as pets?

14 Read

a) Read the text and guess the meaning of these words and phrases. Check your answers with your teacher or a dictionary.

- to crawl   • narrow ledge
- to fear the worst   • to repay

b) Answer the questions.

1 Why was the dog a problem?
2 What did Leif see when he walked into the bedroom?
3 How did the dog rescue the girl?
4 Who had the 'lucky escape'?

15 Over to you

Answer the questions.

Do you think it's cruel to keep big animals in flats?
What animal stories have been in the news lately?

16 Write

Use the story of Stig the Alsatian to help you to write a magazine article about an animal. Use your imagination or write a story which has been in the news recently.

Last winter a man and a woman were walking with their dog near a lake. It was very cold and there was ice on the lake. Suddenly the dog ran ...

Think about these questions.

- What kind of animal was it?
- Where did the story take place?
- Who were the people and what were they doing?
- What did the animal do?
- What reward did it get?

Fast rewind UNITS 8 and 9

Grammar

1> **Complete the sentences with** *did*, *was* **or** *were*.

The sun *was* shining.

1 When ... they arrive?
2 She ... having a good time.
3 They ... n't at school today.
4 I ... n't like her at first.
5 ... they visiting the USA for the first time?
6 ... Gary watching TV all night?

2> **Complete the text with the past simple or past continuous form of the verbs.**

'Last weekend my mother (take) [1] *took* me and my brother on a trip to Blackpool. My father (work) [2] ... so he (not/come) [3] ... with us. We (get up) [4] ... at 5 a.m. on Saturday morning. It (rain) [5] ... when we (leave) [6] ... and my mother (not/feel) [7] ... in a very good mood. After an hour my brother (begin) [8] ... to feel sick so we (stop) [9] ... at a motorway café. Then we (turn off) [10] ... the motorway and (take) [11] ... a small country road. Anyway, we (drive) [12] ... along when suddenly we (see) [13] ... about twenty sheep in the middle of the road. They (just/stand) [14] ... there. We nearly (hit) [15] ... one of them. They (not/move) [16] ... for an hour so we just (sit) [17] ... there! In the end, we (not/get to) [18] ... Blackpool until after lunch.'

3> **Join the parts of the sentences with** *when* **or** *while* **and the correct form of the past tense.**

I/have breakfast ... // the parcel/arrive. (when)
I was having breakfast when the parcel arrived.

... I/wash my hair // someone/knock at the door. (while)
While I was washing my hair, someone knocked at the door.

1 We/just go out ... // it/begin to snow. (when)
2 ... she/swim in the sea // she/lose one of her beach shoes. (while)
3 I/do my homework ... // all the lights/go out. (when)
4 ... they/have dinner // the cat/eat the goldfish. (while)
5 My brother/cycle quite fast ... // he/got a puncture. (when)
6 ... I/change some money // a robber/run into the bank. (while)

Vocabulary

4> **Choose the correct ending to complete the animal words.**

• se • ep • oceros • aroo • ar • fish • rot • en
• affe • ant

1 elephant

1 eleph	3 kang	5 chick	7 gold	9 hor
2 be	4 gir	6 she	8 rhin	10 par

Communication

5> **Use the map to complete the conversation.**

A: Excuse me. Is there a post office [1] ... here?
B: Yes, [2] ... is. It's [3] ... East Street.
A: How do I get to it [4] ... here?
B: Walk [5] ... this street – King Street – and [6] ... at the traffic lights.
A: Those traffic lights over there?
B: That's right. Then take [7] ... right into [8] ... Street.
A: First turning. OK.
B: The post office is about 50 metres down the street on your [9] ... . It's [10] ... the police station.

6> **Work in pairs. Student A:** Ask Student B

• where he/she first went to school.
• what he/she was doing last night at 9 o'clock.
• how much a litre of milk costs.
• how to get to the nearest football ground from school.

Now Student B: Ask Student A

• two things he/she did at the weekend.
• what he/she was doing at 7 o'clock this morning.
• how much a cup of coffee costs.
• how to get to his/her home from school.

Progress update Units 8 and 9

How do you rate your progress? Tick the chart.

	Excellent ★★★★	Good ★★★	OK ★★	Can do better ★
Grammar				
Vocabulary				
Communication				

Into the jaws of...

DANGER

Underwater photographer, John Paterson, tells of the day he came face to face with a great white shark.

'I was snorkelling alone near some islands in the east of the Pacific Ocean. I was coming up from a dive when I saw the shark about six metres away. Suddenly it turned and came towards me through the water like a rocket. I just had time to put my hand up in front of my face. Then the shark hit me with all its force and bit my hand. I didn't actually feel the bite.

My face mask fell off so I couldn't see anything. I swam to the surface and looked for the boat. I screamed the word "Shark!" Then I saw the boat. It was only fifty metres away but it looked like a kilometre.

I swam on my back towards the boat with my bad arm above the water. I was sure that the shark was somewhere near me but I didn't know where. I screamed "Shark!" again and again. My life rolled like a film in front of my eyes.

Shark facts

- There are over 300 species of shark in the world.

- The biggest shark (the enormous whale shark) can be 15 to 20 metres long and the smallest (the pygmy shark) only 60 centimetres long.

- Some sharks are harmless but others, like the grey reef shark and the great white man-eating shark, can be aggressive and attack humans.

My arm was bleeding badly and I left a cloud of blood behind me. Then I saw the black triangle of a fin on the surface of the water. The shark was following me. I knew it was going to bite me again.

The shark came from behind, and bit my right shoulder. I was swimming and screaming. Finally I saw someone in a dinghy. He was rowing towards me from the boat. Just in time, I pulled myself over the side of the dinghy, and I was safe.'

Before you read

Write three questions which you would like to ask about sharks. Then read the text and see if your questions are answered.

1 > Read

a) Read the text and guess the meaning of these words. Check your answers with your teacher or dictionary.

- snorkel (*v.*) • bite (bit) (*v.*) • bite (*n.*) • mask
- fall (fell) off • surface • scream (*v.*) • roll (*v.*)
- bleed • dinghy • row (a boat)

b) Put the events in the correct order to summarise the story.

1 i) John Paterson was snorkelling in the Pacific Ocean.

a) He lost his face mask.
b) He swam towards the boat.
c) The shark bit his shoulder.
d) He tried to protect his face.
e) He managed to reach the dinghy.
f) He saw the shark's fin.
g) He swam up to the surface of the water.
h) The shark bit his hand.
i) John Paterson was snorkelling in the Pacific Ocean.
j) He saw the shark for the first time.

2 > 👀 Listen

Listen to John talking about a frightening incident.

1 Where was he and what was he doing at the time?
2 Which lion were the wardens trying to find and why?
3 What sort of gun were the wardens carrying?
4 What happened?

3 > Write

Write about an accident at the seaside, on the road or at school.

- Say when it happened.
- Describe where you were and what you were doing.
- Say what you saw and what happened.
- Say what you did or what someone else did.
- Describe how you feel about it now.

Project ▶ ② *Snapshot of a famous life*

Choose a famous person and write a project about him/her. Find out about the person's life and make a factfile about them. Use pictures to illustrate your project.

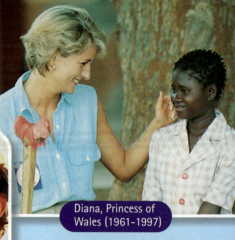
Diana, Princess of Wales (1961-1997)

Martin Luther King, American civil rights leader (1929–1968)

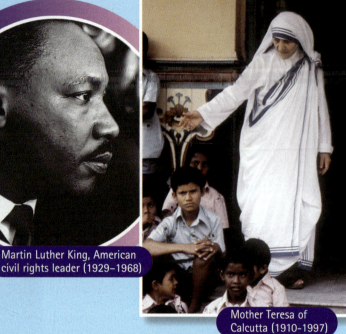
Mother Teresa of Calcutta (1910-1997)

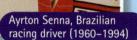
Ayrton Senna, Brazilian racing driver (1960–1994)

Pablo Picasso, Spanish artist (1881–1973)

FACTFILE

Name: **Martin Luther King**
Nationality: **American**
Work: **church minister and civil rights leader**
Dates: **1929-1968**
Achievements: **fought against racial discrimination in the USA**
Key events: **1957: ended 'whites-only' buses in almost every city in the south of the USA**
1963: led a huge civil rights march of over 200,000 people on Washington, where he gave his famous 'I have a dream' speech.
1964: won the Nobel Peace Prize
1968: was shot and killed in Memphis, Tennessee

Write a paragraph about the person's life.

Martin Luther King was an American church minister and civil rights leader who fought against racial discrimination in the USA. In particular, he ended 'whites-only' buses in almost every city in the south of the USA, and he led a huge civil rights march on Washington in 1963. There he gave his famous 'I have a dream' speech. In 1964 he won the Nobel Peace Prize. He was shot and killed in Memphis, Tennessee in 1968 at the age of thirty-nine.

This song was written by John Lennon and Paul McCartney and featured in the Beatles' first album, *Please Please Me*, released in April 1963.

I saw her standing there

Well, she was just seventeen,
You know what I mean,
And the way she looked was way beyond compare,
So how could I dance with another,
oh when I ¹ .... her standing there?
Well, she ² .... at me,
and I, I ³ .... see,
that before too long I'd fall in love with her.
She wouldn't dance with another,
oh when I saw her standing there.

Well, my heart ⁴ .... boom when I ⁵ .... that room,
and I ⁶ .... her hand in mine.
Well, we ⁷ .... through the night,
and we held each other tight,
and before too long I ⁸ .... in love with her.
So I'll never dance with another,
Since I saw her standing there.

Well, my heart .... boom when I .... that room,
and I .... her hand in mine.
Well, we .... through the night,
and we held each other tight,
and before too long I .... in love with her.
So how could I dance with another,
Since I saw her standing there?

1▷ 👀 Read the lyrics of the song and complete the gaps with these verbs in the past tense. Then listen and see if you were right.

• look • hold • dance • see • cross
• fall • go • can

2▷ Find the words in the song which rhyme with these words.

• seventeen • compare • me • night

3▷ Choose the sentence which best describes the song.

a) He was angry with her for only dancing with him once.

b) He was jealous because she was looking at another man.

c) He thought she was very attractive and fell in love with her.

11 I've lost my rucksack.

Learning goals

Communication
Ask about and describe objects
Describe people

Grammar
Present perfect simple
Prepositions: *with*, *on*, *in*

Vocabulary
Materials and personal possessions
Clothes
Physical description

1 > 🔊 Listen and read

The volunteers are going on a day trip to Blackpool.

Spike: Sorry I'm late! Can you hang on a minute? I've lost my rucksack. I've looked everywhere for it.

Mick: Spike, you don't need a rucksack. We're only going on a day trip!

Spike: But I must find it. It's got my camera and a spare T-shirt and lots of other stuff in it.

Mick: When did you last have it?

Spike: I know I had it on Sunday evening at Joe's birthday party. It was with my jacket in the dining room.

Mick: Hey, you lot! Has anyone seen Spike's bag?

Joe: What's it like?

Spike: It's a blue and black rucksack with some stickers on it.

Stefan: Have you asked Stella? Maybe she's put it somewhere.

Gabriel: Stella isn't here. She's gone to town with Katie and Sam.

Spike: Oh, never mind. Let's get going!

Sandra: At last!

2 > Comprehension

a > **Answer T (true), F (false) or DK (don't know).**

1 Spike can't find her rucksack.
2 The rucksack has got Spike's diary in it.
3 Spike lost the rucksack on Sunday morning.
4 Stella is at the hostel.
5 Sandra is pleased when the bus leaves.

b > **Complete Spike's entry on the hostel lost property card.**

Lost property		Date *19th August*
Name and room	Item lost	Description
J. Hunter *Room 8*		
Other details *Contents: camera, ...*	When and where last seen	

3 > 🔊 Useful phrases

Listen and repeat.

- Can you hang on a minute? • Hey, you lot! • What's it like?
- Never mind. • Let's get going! • At last!

Grammar snapshot

Present perfect simple

Positive statements			Negative statements		
I/You We/They	've (have)	seen the bag.	I/You We/They	haven't	seen the diary.
He/She	's (has)		He/She	hasn't	

Questions				Short answers						
				Positive			Negative			
Have	you/we/ they	seen the bag?	Yes,	I/we/ they	have.	No,	I/we/ they	haven't.		
Has	he/she			he/she	has.		he/she	hasn't.		

Make a rule.
To make the present perfect, we use the present simple of the verb … and the past participle of the main verb.

Go back and look.
Find the past participles in the dialogue in Exercise 1.

Regular verbs		
Infinitive	**Past simple**	**Past participle**
ask	asked	asked
look	looked	looked
pass	passed	passed
search	searched	searched
start	started	started
wait	waited	waited

Irregular verbs		
Infinitive	**Past simple**	**Past participle**
be	was	been
do	did	done
go	went	gone
have	had	had
leave	left	left
lose	lost	lost
put	put	put
see	saw	seen
wear	wore	worn

(A full list of irregular verbs is given on page 128.)

Note.
Note the difference between past participles *gone* and *been*:
She's **gone** to town. (She's still in town.)
She's **been** to town. (She's gone and come back./She isn't in town now.)

4> **Help**line

Learn by heart.

It is a good idea to learn irregular verb forms by heart. It helps to divide them into groups: verbs which do not change, e.g. *put*; verbs with one change, e.g. *have*; and verbs with two changes, e.g. *go*. Look at the list of verbs on page 128 and write them in your notebooks in the three different groups.

5> **Practice**

Make conversations using the present perfect.

A: Why is Sue so happy?
B: (She/pass her exams)
She's passed her exams.

1 A: Why are you hungry?
  B: (I/not have breakfast)
2 A: Why can't they come to the cinema?
  B: (They/not do their homework)
3 A: Everyone says *The Lost World* is great.
  B: Really? (We/not see it)
4 A: Why isn't he playing in the match?
  B: (He/leave his football boots at home)
5 A: Does Alan like his new jacket?
  B: I don't know. He (not/wear it yet)

6> 😐 **Sound**bite

The sound / h /

have   **h**aven't
(Look at page 122.)

7 ▷ Vocabulary

Materials and personal possessions

Material	Object
cotton	rucksack
gold	bag
leather	bracelet
metal	buckle
nylon	diary
plastic	keyring
silk	necklace
silver	pencil case
wool (adj. woollen)	personal stereo
wood (adj. wooden)	purse
	strap
	scarf
	wallet
	watch

Use the words in the box and a colour word to describe each object below.

1 It's a silver bracelet with blue moons and stars on it.

8 ▷ Communication

Asking about and describing objects

▶ Excuse me, I've lost my watch. Has anybody handed it in?
▶ What's it like?
▶ It's silver with a black leather strap.
▶ You're lucky. Here it is./No, I'm afraid we've only got a (gold) watch.
▶ Thanks./Oh, OK. Never mind. Thanks.

Now look at the pictures below and ask and answer about the following lost objects.

1 a yellow silk scarf with green flowers on it
2 a purple plastic purse with a picture of The Beatles on it
3 a black pen with a silver top
4 a red leather diary with a black strap
5 a yellow and green nylon rucksack with names
   of football teams on it

9 ▷ Over to you

Describe three personal possessions which you like and three which you don't like.

I've got a green nylon rucksack with a picture of Brad Pitt on it.
I like it very much.
I've got a red plastic watch with Mickey Mouse on it.
I don't like it at all.

10 ▷ 👀 Listen

Listen to the telephone conversation and answer the questions.

1 Describe in detail what the man has found.
2 Where did he find it?
3 What is going to happen?

Lost Friends

Netscape

Netsite: http://www.lost friends.com

What's New? | What's Cool? | Destinations | Net Search | People | Software

Lost Friends

Lost Friends puts you in touch with people you want to contact again.

Has anyone seen Marco?

Your name is Marco. You're seventeen and you've got short brown hair and glasses. You've got a green and black scooter, and you've just taken your exams. My name is Amy and we met at a campsite near Lake Balaton in Hungary on 27th July. You were wearing a blue T-shirt, a grey striped shirt and a checked jacket. We swapped names and addresses and someone took this photo. I've written to you twice but you haven't answered. Have I done something wrong? Please get in touch.

Amy@ajd.telstar.uk

Before you read

Have you ever tried to contact someone on the Internet?

11 > Read

Read the Lost Friends message and copy and complete the information.

Name: *Amy*
Looking for:
Physical description:
What he was wearing:
When and where they met:

12 > Memory bank

Hair colour and style
• blonde • brown • dark
• fair • short • long
• curly • wavy • straight

Eye colour
• blue • brown • green
• grey

13 > Over to you

Close your eyes and describe:

• what you are wearing today.
• what your partner looks like.
• what your partner is wearing.

Clothes
• jacket • jeans • trousers • skirt
• sweater • dress • belt • boots • top
• shoes • T-shirt • pullover • cardigan
• sweatshirt • trainers • shirt

Style of clothes
• baggy • tight • long-sleeved/short-sleeved

14 > Write

Write a Lost Friends entry for the Internet with details of someone you want to contact.

Sam is in trouble

Read the story and try to guess the missing questions. Then listen and see if you were right.

1. Mick, I'm still worried about my rucksack.
   OK. Let's go and phone Stella.

2. That was Mick on the phone. Spike's lost her bag. _____ ?
   No, I haven't. Sorry!

3. Are you sure, Sam?
   Mum! I'm trying to watch this programme. _____ ?

4. It's a blue and black rucksack with some stickers on it.
   Oh, that one!
   What do you mean, 'Oh, that one'? _____ ?

5. It's in the garden.
   The garden? _____ ?

6. We needed a goalpost! We were playing football.
   I don't care what you were doing! Go and get it at once!

12 > It's the highest in the world.

Learning goals

Communication
Ask and talk about experiences
Make comparisons

Grammar
Present perfect simple with *never* and *ever*
Comparative and superlative of short and long adjectives
Question word: *How?* + adjective

Vocabulary
Adjectives of measurement: *fast, heavy, high, long, wide*

1 > 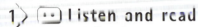 listen and read

Joe:	It says here that *The Big One* is the highest rollercoaster in the world. Are you coming on it, Louise?
Louise:	No, thanks.
Joe:	Why not? Are you frightened?
Louise:	No, of course not. I've been on more frightening rides than that! I'm just not in the mood.
Joe:	Well, I'm going on it.
Louise:	OK. Suit yourself!
Joe:	Have you ever been to Disneyworld, Gabriel?
Gabriel:	No, I haven't. I've never been to the USA. But I've been to Port Aventura.
Joe:	What's that? I've never heard of it.
Gabriel:	It's a theme park near Barcelona.
Joe:	Is it better than this?
Gabriel:	I don't know yet, but it's bigger!
Stefan:	What's that, Spike?
Spike:	Candyfloss. Have you ever tasted it?
Stefan:	No. What's it like?
Spike:	It's very sweet. Here, have a taste.
Stefan:	Mmm. It's nice.

2 > Comprehension

Correct the sentences which are not true.

1 Louise doesn't want to go on the rollercoaster.
2 Louise has been on big rides before.
3 Gabriel has been to Disneyworld.
4 Joe has heard of Port Aventura.
5 Stefan doesn't like the taste of candyfloss.

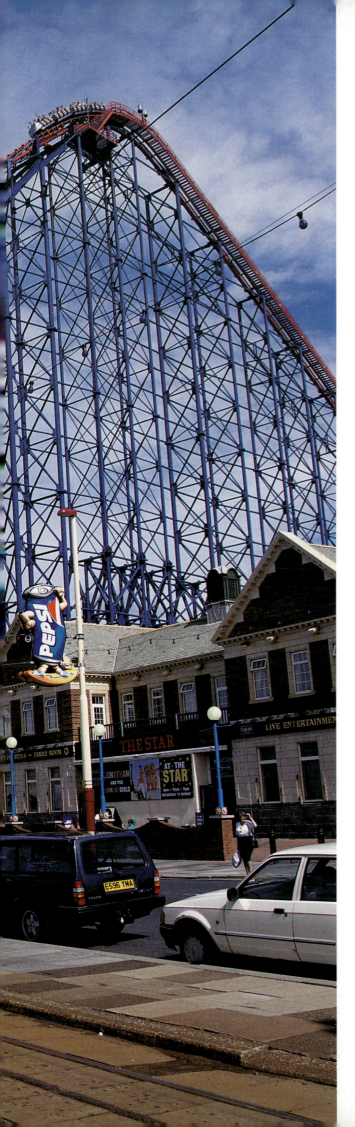

3 > 👀 Useful phrases

Listen and repeat.

- It says here that ...
- Why not?
- No, of course not.
- I'm just not in the mood.

- Suit yourself!
- I've never heard of it.
- I don't know yet.
- Here, have a taste.

Grammar flash

Present perfect simple with *never* **and** *ever*
I've **never** been to Disneyworld.
Have you **ever** been to Disneyworld?

4 > Communication

Asking and talking about experiences

▶ Have you ever been to a theme park?
▶ Yes, I have. I've been to Disneyland Paris.
▶ When did you go?
▶ I went last summer.
▶ What was it like?
▶ It was exciting/fun/horrible/boring/expensive.

▶ Have you ever flown in a helicopter?
▶ No, I haven't but I'd like to./No, I haven't and I don't want to!

Use the prompts to ask and talk about your experiences.

- go to a theme park
- hit anybody
- see anyone famous
- break your arm or leg
- drink goat's milk

- meet anyone famous
- fly in a helicopter/small plane
- act in a play
- play in a band
- eat raw fish

Now tell the class about your partner's experiences.

Carla has been to a theme park. She went last August. It was exciting but very expensive.

5 > Write

Write five sentences about your experiences.

I've never flown in a helicopter but I've been in a small six-seater plane.

Grammar snapshot

The comparative and superlative of short and long adjectives

Adjective	Comparative	Superlative
high	higher	highest
big	bigger	biggest
heavy	heavier	heaviest
frightening	more frightening	most frightening
terrifying	more terrifying	most terrifying

Irregular adjectives

good	better	best
bad	worse	worst
far	further	furthest

The Big One is **faster than/more frightening than** the ride at Port Aventura.
The Big One is **the highest/the most exciting** ride in the world.

6 Soundbite

Sentence stress

It's the <u>long</u>est <u>ride</u> in the <u>world</u>.
(Look at page 123.)

7 Practice

a> Compare the cars, using the comparative form of the adjectives.

estate car/sports car/reliable

The estate car is more reliable than the sports car.

1 sports car/hatchback/expensive
2 estate car/sports car/safe
3 hatchback/sports car/big
4 sports car/estate car/fast
5 sports car/hatchback/exciting
   to drive

b> Complete the questions with the correct superlatives.

Which is ... to drive?
Which is the most exciting to drive?
The sports car. It's got a five-star rating.

1 Which is ... ? The estate car. It's got six seats.
2 Which is ... ? The sports car. It can go at 220 km/h.
3 Which is ... ? The estate car. It costs £22,000.
4 Which is ... ? The hatchback. It's got a four-star rating.
5 Which is ... ? The estate car. It's got a five-star rating for safety.

	Hatchback	Estate car	Sports car
Price	£15,900	£22,000	£19,500
Top speed	180 km/h	200 km/h	220 km/h
Number of seats	4	6	2
Safety (top rating ★★★★★)	★★★	★★★★★	★★
Exciting to drive? (top rating ★★★★★)	★★★	★★	★★★★★
Reliable (top rating ★★★★★)	★★★★	★★★	★★

8 Helpline

Check spelling.

Some English words are often wrongly spelt by students. Rewrite the following words correctly, then check them in a dictionary.
• exiting • intresting • dificult
• beautifull • exspensive
• funnyer • frigtening

9 Over to you

a Make a list of three:
• dangerous sports, e.g.
  bungee jumping, paragliding,
  whitewater rafting
• makes of car
• films or videos which you have seen this year
• TV programmes
• school subjects

b Compare the three things in each category using some of these adjectives.

A: *Bungee jumping is more dangerous than whitewater rafting.*
B: *Yes, but it's more exciting.*
• fast • slow • expensive • cheap • dangerous
• safe • boring • interesting • exciting
• frightening • good • bad • funny • popular
• easy • difficult

10 Listen

Louise has had another phone call from her mother. Listen and answer the questions.

1 Who comforts Louise after the phone call?
2 What's the news?
3 How is the news going to change Louise's career?
4 Who interrupts them?

THE ULTIMATE THRILL

You travel 125 metres to the top in a few seconds. But what goes up must come down ...

from Gary Morgan in Los Angeles

Faster than a Porsche, higher than the Statue of Liberty, *Superman the Escape*, at the Six Flags theme park near Los Angeles, is the world's most terrifying theme park ride.

It climbs to a height of 125 metres and then rushes backwards to earth in 6.5 seconds. The acceleration is faster than a Porsche 911 and is similar to a jet fighter plane taking off. At its top speed it goes at 160 kilometres an hour.

'*Superman the Escape* is the ultimate thrill,' says Larry Bouts, the head of the Six Flags theme park. 'At last people can experience what it is like to fly.'

TECHNICAL DETAILS:

Length of track: 405 metres	**Weight of each car:** 6 tonnes
Height: 125 metres	**Width of each car:** 3 metres
Top speed: 160 km/h	**Length of ride:** 1 minute 30 seconds

11 > Read

Read the text and answer the questions.

1 What's the name of the new ride in California?
2 What's its top speed?

12 > Vocabulary

Adjectives of measurement

In pairs, complete each question with the correct adjective. Then use the technical details to give the answers.

1 A: *How high is the 'Superman the Escape' ride?*
   B: *It's 125 metres.*

- heavy • long (x2) • wide • fast • high

1	height	How ... is the *Superman the Escape* ride?
2	speed	How ... do you go?
3	length	How ... is the track?
4	weight	How ... is each car?
5	width	How ... is each car?
6	duration	How ... does the ride last?

> I liked going up but I hated going down backwards. It was really frightening.

> It was brilliant. I screamed all the way!

> I didn't mind it but my girlfriend was sick.

> It's the greatest! I've never been on anything like it before.

13 > Write

Imagine you are on holiday at the Six Flags theme park near Los Angeles. Write a postcard to a friend describing your ride on 'Superman the Escape'.

Dear ... ,

Here I am at ... . I have just been on ... . It was ... . I've never ... before. You go at ... km an hour. It's more frightening than ... .

See you soon,
Love
... .

Fast rewind UNITS 11 and 12

Grammar

1> Complete the sentences with the correct form of the present perfect simple.

... to Madrid three times. (I/be)
I've been to Madrid three times.

1 ... anybody famous? (you/ever/meet)
2 ... that film. (Sally/see)
3 ... to London. (I/never/be)
4 ... the train. (they/miss)
5 ... this book? (you/read)
6 ... abroad? (your father/ever/work)

2> Complete the dialogue with the past simple or present perfect tense of the verbs.

Ben: What's the matter, Jenny?
Jenny: [1] *I've lost* my passport. (lose)
Ben: When [2] ... you ... it? (last use)
Jenny: When I [3] ... to France last summer. (go)
Ben: Maybe Mum [4] .... it. (see)
        Mum, [5] ... Jenny's passport? (you/see)
Mum: [6] ... in all her drawers? (she/look)
Jenny: It's OK. I [7] ... it. (find)
        It [8] .... in my rucksack all the time! (be)

3> What does 's stand for in the sentences: *is* or *has*?

She's tired. *is*   She's had lunch. *has*
1 It's hot.   4 He's looking for his diary.
2 It's arrived.   5 She's sixteen today.
3 She's lost her bag.   6 It's a great film.

4> Complete the sentences with the correct preposition: *on*, *in* or *with*.

There are some lovely pictures *in* this book.

1 He's got a motorbike ... red and silver stripes ... it.
2 Her jeans have got a big hole ... them.
3 I want to buy a denim jacket ... a star ... the back.
4 I've got a T-shirt ... two parrots ... the back.
5 Laura is the only girl ... red hair ... the class.

5> Complete the sentences with the adjectives in their comparative or superlative forms.

A mile is ... a kilometre. (long)
A mile is longer than a kilometre.

1 I'm ... my father. (tall)
2 What's ... film on at the moment? (frightening)
3 Is Spanish ... French? (easy)
4 The book is ... the film. (interesting)
5 The new Spice Girls CD is ... their last one. (good)
6 The final was ... match of the season. (bad)

Vocabulary

6> Sort the words into three groups: size, material, possessions.

• woollen • rucksack • large • bracelet • deep
• plastic • keyring • leather • wide • cotton • belt
• denim • wallet • long • tall

7> Choose the correct adjective in each sentence.

How *long/far* does it take to get from Oxford to London?

1 Is it very *far/long* from the station to the school?
2 How *tall/high* are you?
3 Don't dive. The swimming pool isn't very *wide/deep*.
4 The window wasn't open very *wide/deep*, but he managed to get in.

Communication

8> Work in pairs. Student A:
Ask Student B
• to describe him/herself and say what he/she is wearing.
• if he/she has ever been to the USA.
• to compare two subjects he/she does at school.

Now Student B:
Ask Student A
• to describe a personal possession.
• if he/she has ever been to Britain.
• to compare two films he/she has seen this month.

Progress update Units 11 and 12

How do you rate your progress? Tick the chart.

	Excellent ★★★★	Good ★★★	OK ★★	Can do better ★
Grammar				
Vocabulary				
Communication				

You shouldn't move it.

Learning goals

Communication
Talk about injuries
Make decisions
Give advice

Grammar
Verb *will/won't* for
   predictions and decisions
Verb *should/shouldn't* for
   advice and obligation

Vocabulary
Parts of the body

1 > Vocabulary

Parts of the body

- arm • finger • hand • ear • hair
- face • stomach • knee • leg
- wrist • hip • mouth • nose
- thumb • toe • shoulder • waist
- neck • back • eye • ankle
- foot (*pl.* feet) • elbow

a> Match the numbers with the parts of the body.

1 – finger.

b> List the words in four groups.

the head	the leg	the arm	the body
ear	*knee*	*finger*	*shoulder*

c> Add any other words you know to the groups.

2 > Practice

a> Which parts of the body can you break, sprain or twist?

You can break your arm or leg.

b> Where do you wear the things in the list below? Make sentences about them using the prepositions *in*, *on* or *round*.

You wear shoes on your feet.

- shoes • earrings • a tie • make-up
- a scarf • gloves • tights • a ring
- a watch • a hat • a ribbon
- a rucksack • a belt

3 〉 👀 Listen and read

Louise: What a view!
Joe: I'll take a photo. Say 'cheese'!
Sandra: Joe! Look out!

Louise: Are you OK, Joe?
Joe: I've hurt my ankle. It's very painful. I think I've sprained it.
Spike: You shouldn't ride on these paths. They're not race tracks, you know.
Boy: I didn't think there was anyone up here.
Louise: You didn't think. Full stop.
Joe: I'll try and walk on it.
Sandra: No, no. You shouldn't put any weight on it. Perhaps we should take him to hospital.
Boy: I'll go and get help. There's a farmhouse down there.
Stefan: No, hang on. I've got an idea. Gabriel, join hands with me and we'll make a seat. We'll carry him to the farmhouse.
Gabriel: OK. All right, Joe? It won't be long now.
Louise: Will he be all right?
Spike: Don't worry. He'll be fine.

4 〉 Comprehension

Answer the questions.

1 What part of his body did Joe hurt?
2 Where was the boy on the motorbike riding?
3 What did the boy offer to do?
4 How did Joe get to the farmhouse?

5 〉 👀 Useful phrases

Listen and repeat.

- What a view!
- Say 'cheese'!
- Look out!
- Full stop.
- I've got an idea.
- All right, [Joe]?
- Don't worry.

Grammar snapshot

Verb *will*/*won't* **for predictions and decisions**

Positive statements
I'll (I will) take a photo.
We'll (we will) carry him.

Negative statements
It won't (will not) be long.

Question

Will he be all right?

Short form answers

Positive	Negative
Yes, he will.	No, he won't.

Note.
Will and *won't* are the same for all persons.

6 ⚄ **Sound**bite   The sound / l /

I'll   he'll   (Look at page 123.)

7 Practice

Complete the conversation using *will*, *'ll* **or** *won't*.

Tim: I want to go walking with Ruth in the Lake District.
          Is that OK?
Father: The Lake District? That's a long way. How (you get) ¹ ...
          there?
Tim: We (go) ² ... by bus. It (not take) ³ ... very long.
Father: What time (you be) ⁴ ... back?
Tim: I don't know but we (not/be) ⁵ ... very late.
Father: Fine. I (keep) ⁶ ... some supper for you.
Tim: Thanks.
Father: Now, (you be) ⁷ ... all right?
Tim: Of course we ⁸ ...! Don't worry about us. We (be) ⁹ ... fine!

8 **Help**line

Practise speaking.

1 In 'Communication' exercises,
   always change parts at the end
   to get as much practice as
   possible.
2 In freer-speaking practice
   don't worry too much about
   making mistakes.

9 Communication

**Talking about injuries and
making decisions**

▶ What's the matter?
▶ I've twisted my ankle.
▶ Is it very painful?
▶ Yes, it is.
▶ OK. I'll call a doctor.

**Now use the cues to make
similar conversations.**

Injury	Part of the body
• twisted	• finger
• hurt	• wrist
• cut	• ankle
• broken	• knee
• sprained	• hand

Decision
• get some help
• call a doctor
• get a bandage
• put a plaster on it
• get an ice pack

10 Over to you

**Talk about these questions with
your friends.**

1 Have you ever had an
   accident?
2 What part of your body did
   you hurt?
3 Did you go to hospital?
4 Have you got a scar anywhere?
   How did you get it?

Grammar snapshot

Verb *should*/*shouldn't* **for advice and obligation**

Positive statements	Negative statements
We should take him to hospital.	He shouldn't put any weight on it.

Questions

Should we call a doctor?

Short answers

Positive	Negative
Yes, we should.	No, we shouldn't.

Notes.

1 *Should* and *shouldn't* are the same for all persons.

2 *Should* is not as strong as *must*.

11> Practice

Choose two phrases to talk about each picture below using *should* **or** *shouldn't*.

1 He shouldn't take the lift. He should walk up the stairs.

- get up and go out • watch TV • drop litter • read a book
- eat fruit instead • lie in bed all day • eat biscuits
- put it in a bin • take the lift • read in the dark
- turn the light on • walk up the stairs

12> Over to you

Talk about these questions.

Do you know what to do if someone twists their ankle, gets a black eye or faints?

Which of the comments below are right and which are wrong?

1 Ankle injury
A: 'We should keep her ankle on the floor.'
B: 'Let's put an ice pack on her ankle.'

2 Black eye
A: 'I think five minutes is long enough for the compress.'
B: 'We should put some raw steak on his eye.'

3 Fainting
A: 'You should lie down and open the window.'
B: 'I'll try to give her some orange juice.'

Look at page 121 and check your answers.

13 ▷ Read

Read and complete the questionnaire.

14 ▷ Write

Write a Good Date Guide for a boy or a girl.

1 You should never be late on a first date.

Do GOOD MANNERS
matter any more?

Put A, B or C in the boxes to rate the statements.

A = important
B = old-fashioned but OK
C = silly

On public transport you should:

- never put your feet on the seats. ☐
- give your seat to older people. ☐
- never drop chewing gum on the floor. ☐

At school you should:

- always stand up when your teacher comes into the room. ☐
- always stand up when you answer your teacher's questions. ☐
- always call your teacher *Sir* or *Miss*. ☐
- never chew gum when talking to your teacher. ☐

Mainly for boys – you should:

- hold a door open for a girl. ☐
- raise your hat when you meet a girl in the street. ☐
- always tell a girl that she looks nice. ☐
- never kiss a girl on your first date. ☐

Mainly for girls – you should:

- never tease boys about their looks. ☐
- never laugh at a boy's mistakes. ☐
- always offer to pay your share. ☐
- dress nicely when you go out on a date. ☐

How you scored

Mostly As: — You have very good manners but you are almost too good to be true. You can relax a little sometimes!

More As and Bs than Cs: — You are always polite. You probably have a lot of friends. Keep up the good work. You make the world a better place.

Mostly Cs: — Where are your manners - in the litter bin? Maybe you think you are still living in the Stone Age. Try to be a bit more polite to people.

Joe goes to hospital

Read the story and try to guess the missing words. Then listen and see if you were right.

My name's Joe Phillips. I've ____ .

OK. I'll just take some details.

Take a seat. The doctor ____ .

Thank you.

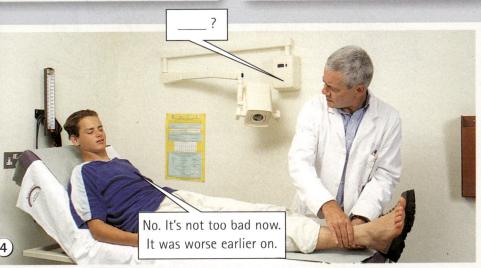

____ ?

No. It's not too bad now. It was worse earlier on.

Do you think I've broken it?

No. I think ____ . We'll take an X-ray just to make sure.

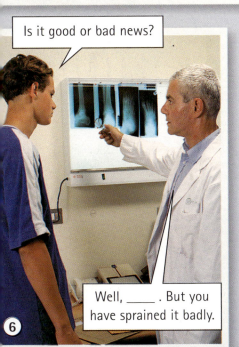

Is it good or bad news?

Well, ____ . But you have sprained it badly.

Can I walk on it?

No. ____ rest it as much as possible.

____ , Joe?

Yes, don't worry. I'm fine.

81

14 ▷ Do I have to?

Learning goals

Communication
Talk about jobs

Grammar
Verb *have to* (present and past simple)

Vocabulary
Household jobs
Occupations

1▷ Vocabulary Household jobs

Use the verb phrases in the box to say what each person is doing.

1 She's making the bed.

> • do the washing • clear the table • do the vacuuming
> • do the shopping • do the washing-up • do the cooking
> • make the bed • do the cleaning • do the ironing • tidy up

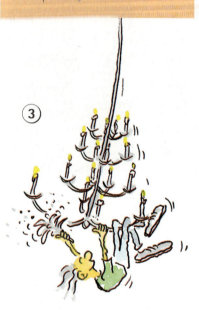

Crosstalk

by Jenny Carstairs

Parents v. Children

In this week's Crosstalk, we talk to Lucy Johnson, 15, and her mother, Mrs Amanda Johnson. Amanda has a full-time job as a school secretary and she expects Lucy and her brother Marcus to help in the house.

LUCY

'I think housework is a waste of time! I don't mind doing the vacuuming or emptying the rubbish, but I really hate cleaning the bathroom and doing the washing-up. I have to clean the bathroom once a week and I also have to do the washing-up every evening. It really gets on my nerves.

Mum says my bedroom is very untidy but I don't think it's a problem. OK, there are some clothes on the floor but it's my room. I say to her "Shut the door and don't worry. I'll tidy it up next week."

My brother Marcus doesn't have to do very much at home. He posts Mum's letters and he waters the plants, but that's not difficult. He sometimes has to help me clear the table and do the washing-up. But when we do the washing-up together, he just washes one or two cups and then runs up to his room.'

LUCY'S MOTHER

'I don't mind doing all the cooking, the washing and the ironing, but I am certainly not going to do everything. When I want Lucy to do something, I sometimes have to ask her three or four times. She often just refuses, or goes off in a huff.

Her bedroom is very untidy. There are a lot of smells in there – food, old cups of coffee and trainers. The strongest smell is her perfume. It's strong enough to cause an explosion!

She says her brother Marcus doesn't have to do much. Well, he's younger than she is, so he only does small jobs. I worry about Lucy. What is she going to be like when she's older and she's got a place of her own?'

2 Read and listen

Read the magazine article. Then listen to Lucy and her mother.

3 Comprehension

Make a list of all the jobs which Lucy and Marcus do to help their mother.

4 Useful phrases

Listen and repeat.

- It's a waste of time.
- It gets on my nerves.
- [She] goes off in a huff.

Grammar snapshot

Verb *have to* present simple

Positive statements

| I have to | tidy up. |
| She has to | |

Negative statements

| I don't have to | empty the rubbish |
| She doesn't have to | |

Questions

| Do you have to | tidy up? |
| Does she have to | |

Short answers

Positive	Negative
Yes, I do.	No, I don't.
Yes, she does.	No, she doesn't

Make similar statements, questions and short answers with *he* and *they*.

Name	Tanya Lane	Rory Grant	Ray Sharman	Jenny Trim
Job	In a children's play group	?	At the post office	?
Duties	Taking the children to the park Tidying up toys	?	Sorting the letters for delivery Working in the parcels collection office	?
Uniform	No	?	Blue shirt, navy blue tie and trousers	?
Hours	8.30–3.30	?	6.00–2.00	?

7 Interaction

Student B: Turn to page 121.

Student A: Find out from Student B about the jobs Rory and Jenny are doing on work experience and complete the chart. Then answer Student B's questions.

A: *Where is Rory doing work experience?*
B: *At a hospital.*
A: *What does he have to do?*
B: *...*
A: *Does he have to wear a uniform?*
B: *...*
A: *What time does he have to start?*
B: *...*

5 Practice

a⟩ Use the list you made in Exercise 3 to say what jobs Lucy has to do at home.

Lucy has to clean the bathroom and do the washing-up. She also ... .

b⟩ Ask and answer about the jobs which Marcus has to do.

A: *Does Marcus have to ...?*
B: *Yes, he does. / No, he doesn't. / I don't know.*

- make his bed
- tidy his room
- do the washing-up
- post the letters
- water the plants

6 Over to you

a⟩ Make lists of the jobs you have to do and those you don't have to do at home.

Which jobs: • do you hate doing?
• really get on your nerves?
• don't you mind doing?

b⟩ Find out the jobs your partner has to do. Are they the same as the jobs you have to do?

A: *Do you have to make your bed?*
B: *Yes, I do. / No, I don't.*

I have to:
make my bed
empty the rubbish

I don't have to:
cook any meals
do the shopping

Tanya

Ray

Grammar snapshot

Verb *have to* **past simple**

Positive

I had to do my homework last night.

Negative

I didn't have to tidy up my room.

Question

Did you have to do your homework?

Short answers

Positive	Negative
Yes, I did.	No, I didn't.

8> Practice

Complete the dialogue with the correct past form of *have to.*

Nicky: Where did you work last week?

Craig: At a supermarket.

Nicky: What ¹*did you have to* do?

Craig: I ²... put things on shelves.

Nicky: Is that all? What else ³... do?

Craig: I ⁴... collect all the trolleys and put them back at the entrance.

Nicky: What time ⁵... start in the morning?

Craig: At 8 o'clock. So I ⁶... get up at 6.30. Can you believe it!

Nicky: What time did you finish?

Craig: At 4 o'clock.

Nicky: ⁷... wear a uniform?

Craig: Yes, ⁸... . That's the worst part. I ⁹... wear a red nylon jacket and black trousers.

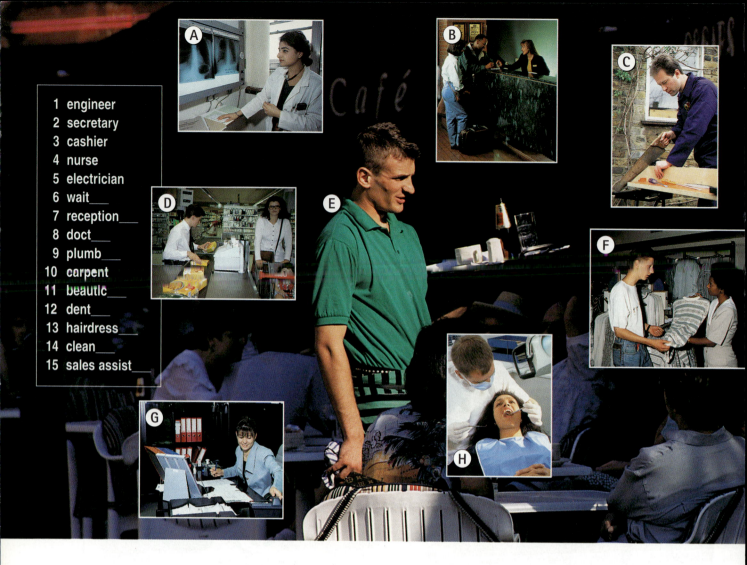

1 engineer
2 secretary
3 cashier
4 nurse
5 electrician
6 wait___
7 reception___
8 doct___
9 plumb___
10 carpent___
11 beautic___
12 dent___
13 hairdress___
14 clean___
15 sales assist___

9 > Vocabulary

Occupations

Choose the correct ending to complete the occupations in the list above.

• -er • -or • -ian • -ist • -ant

Now match each picture with an occupation.

10 > 📼 Soundbite

Word stress

doctor   beautician   (Look at page 123.)

11 > Communication

Talking about jobs

▶ What does your father do?
▶ He's an electrician. He's got his own business.
▶ What does your mother do?
▶ She's a hairdresser. She works in a beauty salon.
▶ What about your brother?
▶ He hasn't got a job. He's still at school.

Now talk about your family.

12 > Helpline

Improve your listening skills.

When you listen to a cassette in class:
1 Look first at the task in your book and think about what you are going to hear.
2 Try to listen for the main ideas first. Don't worry if you do not understand every word.
3 Focus on the words with the main stress. These are often the important words.

Now use the Helpline tips to help you understand Exercise 13.

13 > 📼 Listen

Listen to Anne talking about an amusing incident and answer the questions.

1 When did the incident happen?
2 What did Anne and her friends have to do?
3 Describe the curtains in the two rooms.
4 Why did the girl in the Superstore laugh at Anne?

Grammar

1> **Complete these sentences with** *will,* *'ll* **or** *won't.*

Will you be home before six o' clock?

1 We're really busy, so we ... go out tonight.
2 Excuse me, where ... I find a copy of last week's *Smash Hits?*
3 There aren't any sandwiches left so I ... have a biscuit.
4 I ... have any more coffee, thanks. I've got a headache.
5 The city centre has really changed. You ... be surprised!
6 The children aren't hungry so they ... have anything to eat.

2> **Complete the conversation with** *will,* *'ll* **or** *won't* **and the verb in brackets.**

Jill: Do you want to come to the tennis club disco on Saturday? It (be) [1] *'ll be* good.
Tim: OK. What time does it start?
Jill: Seven thirty.
Tim: Fine. I (meet) [2] ... you at your house at six thirty.
Jill: Promise you (not/be) [3] ... late.
Tim: No, I [4] ... .
Jill: (you/come) [5] ... by bus?
Tim: No, I [6] ... . My cousin (give) [7] ... me a lift.
Jill: OK. I (see) [8] ... you at six thirty.

3> **Complete the advice with** *should* **or** *shouldn't.*

You *should* look both ways before you cross the road.

1 You ... eat with your mouth full.
2 She ... cycle without lights.
3 You ... eat at least one piece of fruit a day.
4 They ... train harder if they want to win.
5 You ... try to answer every question in the exam.
6 People ... throw litter on the streets.

4> **Complete the sentences with the correct form of** *have to.*

The students at summer camp *have to* get up at 6 a.m.

1 You ... (not) go if you don't want to.
2 ... you ... stand up when you speak to your teacher in class?
3 She ... (not) wear a uniform when she went to summer school in Spain.
4 He's hurt his arm so he ... go to hospital for an X-ray.
5 ... people ... get a visa for a trip to Australia?
6 ... he ... to drive on a motorway when he took his driving test?

Vocabulary

5> **Choose the odd word in each group.**

	hand	finger	waist	wrist
1	ankle	arm	foot	knee
2	finger	eye	ear	mouth
3	shoulder	hip	back	toe
4	ear	thumb	eye	nose

6> **Match the name of the job with the symbol.**

• waiter • electrician • doctor • hairdresser • carpenter

Communication

7> **Work in pairs. Student A:**

Ask Student B

• what you should do (you've cut your finger).
• to make a prediction about his/her favourite sports star or team.
• about some of the household jobs he/she has to do.
• about his/her father's or mother's job.

Now Student B:

Ask Student A

• what you should do (you've got a black eye).
• to make a prediction about his/her favourite TV personality or show.
• about a household job he/she has to do but hates doing.
• about his/her father's or mother's job.

Progress update Units 13 and 14

How do you rate your progress? Tick the chart.

	Excellent ★★★★	Good ★★★	OK ★★	Can do better ★
Grammar				
Vocabulary				
Communication				

Too old at fourteen?

Josh advises an American multinational company on what's cool. He is nearly at the end of his working life. Josh is nearly fourteen.

① Joshua Koplewicz from New York is a consultant who advises a multinational jeans company on what's in and what's out and what kind of things American teenagers want. He has already changed the way the world looks, or at least, the way the world dresses.

② American teenagers spend more than 100 billion dollars a year. So it's no surprise that big companies want to find out what teenagers want. Many companies have 'focus groups': groups of teenagers who give their opinions on products like clothes, food, computer games and software. Some companies also employ specialist consultants like Josh.

③ The people at the jeans company noticed Josh's sense of style two years ago when they interviewed him as part of a survey of teenage fashions. They asked Josh over 100 questions about things like where a button or a pocket should go, or what kind of sports and games are cool to play.

④ The company liked his answers and they hired him to do a number of research projects every year. "The company gave me a camera, a tape recorder and a notebook. I had to interview kids who I thought were cool. Once I had to write imaginary letters to kids in Russia about the kind of things that American teenagers were wearing and doing."

⑤ The job is quite hard work but the company pay him well. "It's much better than baby-sitting," laughs Josh. "I have already earned ten times my weekly pocket money for only twenty hours' work!"

⑥ However Josh's job is not secure. The company asked him a few months ago to give them the names of some 'stylish' kids who were three years younger than him and Josh knew that his present job was coming to an end. "They haven't phoned me for some time. I think I'm too old!"

1 Read

a) Read about a teenage consultant. In which paragraph is each question answered?
a) Does Josh earn a lot of money?
b) When did he have his first interview with the company?
c) What sort of company does he work for?
d) Will Josh have the job for a long time?
e) What equipment did the company give him?
f) Why are young people employed by big companies?

b) Now answer the questions above.

2 Listen

Listen to two young people talking about how they earn or earned pocket money. Then complete the notes.

	Charlie	Rachel
Type of work?		
How often?		
How much money?		

3 Speak

Mark the statements on a scale from 1 to 5. Then compare your ratings with your friends.
1 = I don't agree at all ⟶ 5 = I agree strongly
1 It is OK for teenagers to earn some money while they are at school.
2 It is important to wear the latest fashion.
3 It is a good idea for companies to use teenagers as consultants.
4 Companies should pay teenage consultants the same amount of money that they pay adults.

4 Write

Write a letter to some teenagers in another country. Tell them 'what's in and what's out' at the moment among you and your friends. Think about:
- clothes
- TV
- food and drink
- sports and games

Project ③ Snapshot of my experiences

Write a project about your recent experiences. Choose two of the following topics and write a short description. Find pictures to illustrate your project.
- Interesting places you have visited
- Some interesting books you have read
- Something exciting or unusual you have done
- A celebration you have had
- A sports event you have watched or taken part in
- Someone important you have seen

Interesting places I've visited

This summer we went on a camping holiday to southern Italy. I've been to Italy before but this holiday was better than the last one. One day we went to Pompeii, near Naples. Pompeii is an ancient Roman city which was buried in ash in A.D. 78 when the volcano Vesuvius erupted. You can see the remains of Roman streets, shops and houses. These show you daily life in an ancient city.

We also went to the Isle of Capri. We took a boat to see the Blue Grotto. It's a huge cave and the water is incredibly blue and clear. I've never seen anything so beautiful in my whole life.

Interesting books I've read

I've just read Stephen King's horror novel 'The Shining'. It's about a boy with special powers and the things that happen while his parents are looking after a haunted hotel in the Rocky Mountains when it is closed for the winter. It's very long but it's good. It's more frightening than 'Dracula' by Bram Stoker because it's modern. I've also seen the film of 'The Shining'. The book is more frightening than the film because you use your imagination.

Take a break

Love is all around

Love is all around was a hit in 1967 for a British rock group, The Troggs. Nearly thirty years later, the song was a hit for a second time when it was featured in the film *Four Weddings and a Funeral*, which was a big success in 1994. The song remained in the charts for many weeks.

I feel it in my fingers,
I feel it in my [1] ....
The love that's all around me,
And so the feeling [2] ....

It's written on the wind,
It's everywhere I [3] ....,
Oh, yes, it is!
So if you really love me,
Come on and let it [4] ....
Oh, yeah!

You know I love you, I always will,
My mind's made up by the way that I feel.
There's no beginning, there'll be no [5] .... ,
'cause on my love you can [6] ....
Ooh

I see your face before me
As I lay on my [7] ....;
I cannot get to thinking
Of all the things you [8] ....
Oh, yes, I do.

You gave your promise to me
And I gave mine to [9] ....;
I need someone beside me
In everything I [10] ....
Oh, yes, I do.

You know I love you, I always will,
My mind's made up by the way that I feel.
There's no beginning, there'll be no ....,
'cause on my love you can ....
Got to keep it moving, yes!

It's written on the wind.
It's everywhere I ....
Yes, yes. Ooh!
So if you really love ....,
Love me, just let it ....
Come on and let it ....

1> 👀 Find the pairs of words below which rhyme and put them in the correct places in the song. Then listen and see if you were right.
• grows • you • end • go • bed • said
• depend • show • do • toes

2> How many words for parts of the body can you find in the song? List them.

91

16 What would you like to do?

What's on in **Liverpool**

• concert

mus

16th-23rd August

MOSCOW STATE CIRCUS

There's only one Moscow State Circus! This is a once-in-a-lifetime opportunity for young and old to see one of the greatest shows on earth, with clowns, acrobats and beautiful animals.
Sefton Park

Summer Pops Series of popular classical concerts including Vivaldi's *Four Seasons*, Mozart's *Eine Kleine Nachtmusik* and Beethoven's *Fifth Symphony*, performed by Liverpool's world class orchestra.
Conductor: Sir Simon Rattle.
Liverpool Town Hall

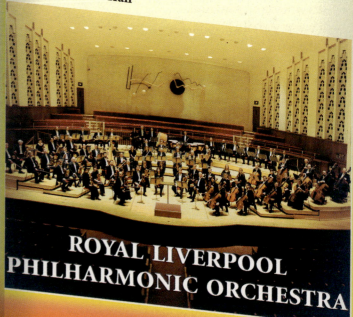

ROYAL LIVERPOOL PHILHARMONIC ORCHESTRA

1> Comprehension

Which events would be interesting for someone who likes the things below?

- classical music
- dance
- art
- musicals
- acrobatics

2> 🔊 Listen

a> **Listen to** *What's on in Liverpool?* **and list the events in the order the presenters talk about them.**

b> **Listen again and answer the questions.**

1 How many days is the dance festival?
2 What time does *Rent* start?
3 What day of the week is the Liverpool Philharmonic concert?
4 What is special about the Goya exhibition?
5 What is one of the special acts at the circus?

- plays
- circus
- concerts
- exhibitions
- musicals
- plays
- circu

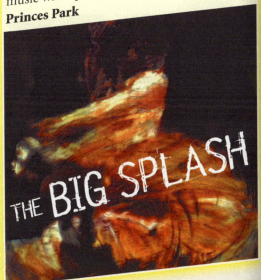

A festival of Latin American and Caribbean music with spectacular displays of dancing.
Princes Park

THE BIG SPLASH

GOYA EXHIBITION

n exhibition of paintings by Goya, the famous Spanish artist.
he Walker Art Gallery

The musical RENT
Don't miss this wonderful 90s rock musical, inspired by Puccini's classic opera *La Bohème*.
'*Rent* is the best show in years.' (*Variety*)
'It's big, it's funny, it's sad and it's got some great music!' (*Liverpool Echo*)
The Liverpool Empire

3 ⊙ Listen and read

Mick: Have you all seen the list of *What's on in Liverpool*?
Spike: Yes, we have, thanks.
Mick: So ... What would you like to do on Saturday?
Gabriel: I'd like to go to the Goya exhibition.
Spike: Me too.
Stefan: And me.
Louise: I'd rather go to the dance festival.
Mick: Joe? What about you?
Joe: I'd prefer to go to the dance festival, too.
Mick: So nobody wants to go to the circus?
Gabriel: No, thanks.
Mick: OK, everyone. What about Saturday evening? Would you like to go to the concert or go to the theatre to see *Rent*?
All: Go to the theatre!
Mick: All right but don't be disappointed if I can't get tickets. It's a very popular show. See you all at supper!
Louise: OK. What shall we do now? I feel like some exercise. How's your ankle, Joe?
Joe: It's better, thanks. Why don't we go for a walk?
Louise: Yes, I'd love to.

4 Comprehension

Complete Mick's booking list.

Event	Name
1 Classical music concert	*Nobody*
2 Art exhibition	
3 Dance festival	
4 Theatre visit	
5 The circus	

5 ⊙ Useful phrases

Listen and repeat.

- So ...
- I feel like [some exercise].
- Yes, I'd love to.

6 Soundbite

I like / aɪˈlaɪk / and I'd like / aɪdˈlaɪk /
I like your jacket.   I'd like your jacket.
(Look at page 123.)

7 Memory bank

Leisure activities

- a concert • bowling • a party • sightseeing
- a basketball match • the sports centre
- swimming • sailing • the theatre • cycling
- the cinema • the beach • a wildlife park
- a games arcade • line-skating • go-karting
- a disco • a picnic • the circus • ice-skating
- a barbecue • shopping • a football match

a〉 Group the words under the following three
verbs. Some words can go in more than one group.

go to	go	have
a concert	*bowling*	*a party*

b〉 Which activities are better for the evening?

Grammar flash

would rather/would prefer to

I/He They	'd (would) rather go bowling.

I/He They	'd (would) prefer to go cycling.

Make rules by choosing *with* **or** *without*.

1 *Would rather* is followed by a verb in the infinitive
  with/without *to*.
2 *Would prefer* is followed by a verb in the infinitive
  with/without *to*.

8 Communication

**Asking for suggestions, making suggestions and
expressing preferences**

▶ What shall we do on Saturday evening?
▶ Why don't we go bowling?
▶ No, not bowling. I'd rather/prefer to go to a disco
  or the cinema.
▶ Yes, I'd like to go to the cinema.
▶ OK. Let's see what's on.

**In groups of four, use the leisure activities in the
Memory bank and some ideas of your own to
discuss what to do on Saturday or Sunday.**

9 Write

**Write and send a message to a friend to ask if
he/she would like to go with you to a show or an
event in your town.**

From: Max Brown
To: Katie Allan
Date: 24th October

Dear Katie,
Would you like to come with me to see David
Copperfield (the magician) at Earls Court next
week? I saw him on TV and he's very good. If
you want to go, could you phone me this
evening and I'll try to get some tickets.

Max

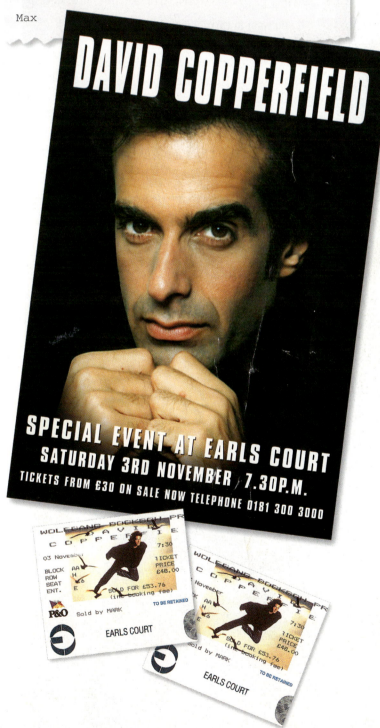

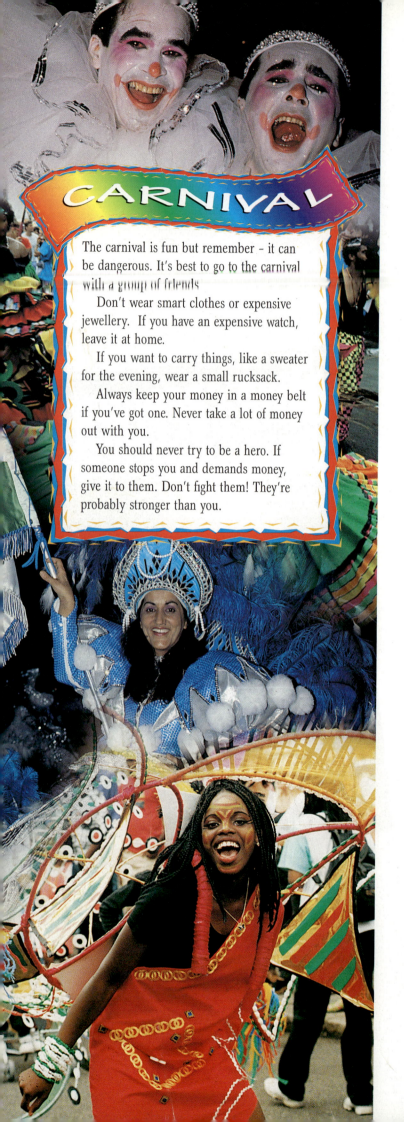

CARNIVAL

The carnival is fun but remember - it can be dangerous. It's best to go to the carnival with a group of friends.

Don't wear smart clothes or expensive jewellery. If you have an expensive watch, leave it at home.

If you want to carry things, like a sweater for the evening, wear a small rucksack.

Always keep your money in a money belt if you've got one. Never take a lot of money out with you.

You should never try to be a hero. If someone stops you and demands money, give it to them. Don't fight them! They're probably stronger than you.

10 > Read

Read about the carnival and look at the pictures. Are the people doing the right (✓) or wrong (✗) things?

Grammar flash

The imperative for instructions and advice
Always keep your money in a money belt.
Never take a lot of money with you.
Don't wear expensive jewellery.

---

11 > Over to you

Talk about these questions.

Do you have a festival or a carnival in your city? If so, what time of year is it? Is it ever dangerous? What advice would you give to visitors?

Always/Never/Don't ... .
You should/shouldn't ... .

12 > **Help**line

Use a dictionary (2).

A good dictionary shows you:
1 how to pronounce a word.
2 what part of speech it is.
3 the meaning of the word.
4 an example of how the word is used.

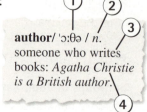

author/ ˈɔːθə / n. someone who writes books: *Agatha Christie is a British author.*

At the theatre

Read the story and try to guess the missing words. Then listen and see if you were right.

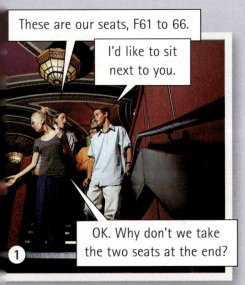

1. These are our seats, F61 to 66.
   I'd like to sit next to you.
   OK. Why don't we take the two seats at the end?

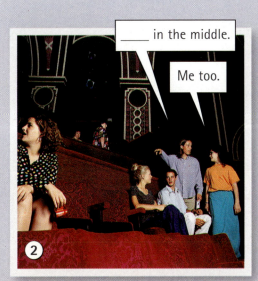

2. _____ in the middle.
   Me too.

3. I'm going to get a programme. _____ ?
   Yes, please.

4. _____ , Sandra, and your change.
   Thank you, Joe.

5. _____ ?
   Yes, OK. Thanks.

6. I told my Dad about your father.
   Why? _____ do?
   He works for a computer company.

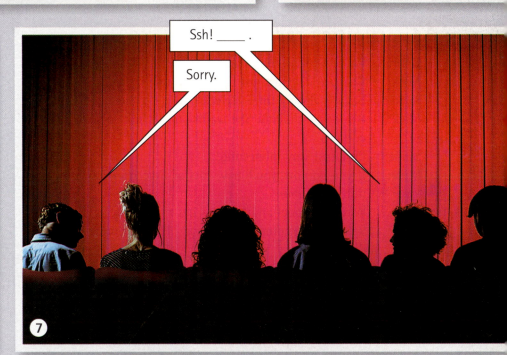

7. Ssh! _____ .
   Sorry.

97

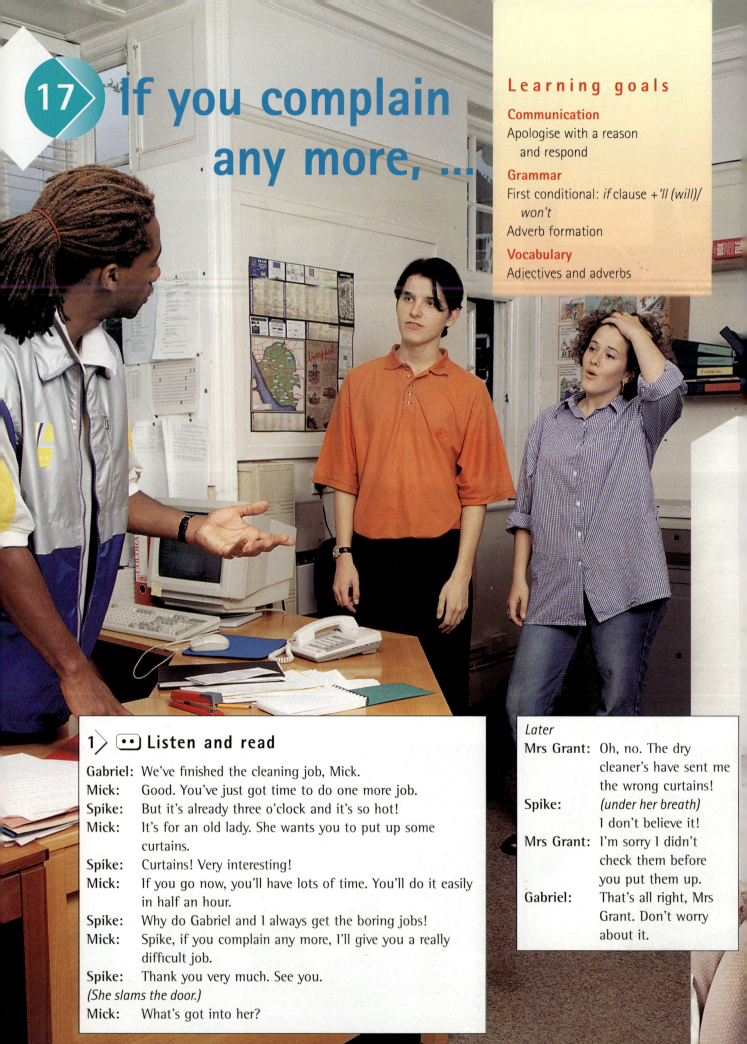

Learning goals

Communication
Apologise with a reason and respond

Grammar
First conditional: *if* clause + *'ll (will)/ won't*
Adverb formation

Vocabulary
Adjectives and adverbs

1 > 👀 Listen and read

Gabriel: We've finished the cleaning job, Mick.
Mick: Good. You've just got time to do one more job.
Spike: But it's already three o'clock and it's so hot!
Mick: It's for an old lady. She wants you to put up some curtains.
Spike: Curtains! Very interesting!
Mick: If you go now, you'll have lots of time. You'll do it easily in half an hour.
Spike: Why do Gabriel and I always get the boring jobs!
Mick: Spike, if you complain any more, I'll give you a really difficult job.
Spike: Thank you very much. See you.
(She slams the door.)
Mick: What's got into her?

Later
Mrs Grant: Oh, no. The dry cleaner's have sent me the wrong curtains!
Spike: *(under her breath)* I don't believe it!
Mrs Grant: I'm sorry I didn't check them before you put them up.
Gabriel: That's all right, Mrs Grant. Don't worry about it.

2 Comprehension

Answer T (true), F (false) or DK (don't know).

1 The cleaning job was easy.
2 Mick has another job for Spike and Gabriel.
3 The weather is quite cold.
4 Spike is in a good mood.
5 Mrs Grant lives alone.
6 The curtains aren't Mrs Grant's.

3 Useful phrases

Listen and repeat.

- It's so hot! • See you. • What's got into [her]?
- I don't believe it!

4 Vocabulary

Adjectives and adverbs

Regular		Irregular	
Adjective	**Adverb**	**Adjective**	**Adverb**
angry	angrily	early	early
bad	badly	fast	fast
careful	carefully	good	well
loud	loudly	hard	hard
quick	quickly	late	late
slow	slowly		
terrible	terribly		

Make a similar chart for these regular adjectives and write the adverbs.

- beautiful • careless • cheap • easy
- (un)happy • quiet • sad • (un)tidy

5 Practice

Complete the sentences with the correct adverb from Exercise 4.

I hate getting up ... .
I hate getting up early.

1 Please talk ... in the library.
2 Remember to read the instructions ... .
3 He was driving too ... when the police caught him.
4 He did ... in the Maths exam. He only got two answers correct.
5 Susie's studying very ... for her exams.
6 I don't understand, so please speak ... .

6 Over to you

Answer the questions below about yourself. Then check and see if your partner agrees.

A: *(I think) I write tidily. Do you agree?*
B: *Yes, I do. / No, I'm afraid I don't. I think you write very untidily!*

Do you:

- write tidily or untidily?
- speak loudly or quietly?
- usually arrive late or early for everything?
- do things carefully or carelessly?
- like films to end happily or sadly?
- sing badly or well?
- eat quickly or slowly?

Grammar snapshot

First conditional *if* clause + *'ll* (*will*) / *won't*

If clause	Main clause
If you complain any more,	I'll (will) give you a really difficult job.
If you go now,	it won't (will not) take long.

Note

The clauses can be reversed: *If you go now, it won't take long./ It won't take long if you go now.*

Make a rule.

In first conditional sentences, the verb in the *if* clause is in the ... tense and the verb in the main clause is in the future tense.

7 ⊡ Sound**bite**

Intonation in conditional sentences

If you go *now*, you'll have lots of *time*.

(Look at page 124.)

8 Practice

Use the cues in each picture to say what the people are thinking.

Giles is waiting for a phone call from a girl he has met at a party.

9 > Communication

Apologising with a reason and responding

▶ I'm sorry I didn't phone you last night. I was really busy.

▶ Never mind. It doesn't matter.

▶ Sorry I forgot your birthday. I lost my diary last week.

▶ That's OK. Don't worry about it.

In pairs, apologise in the following situations and give a reason. You:

• didn't do your homework last night.
• missed a goal in an important match.
• forgot to phone your best friend.
• haven't got your Maths textbook.

4

Can you go and get a pizza for supper?

Must I?

(go out/miss her call completely)

Hi, Giles, Linda here. Would you like to go to the school disco with me on Saturday?

Uh ... uh ... er ... er ...

OK. Never mind.

(he not want to come/ask someone else)

7

(I don't believe it! I've blown it again!)

10 > Write

Send a message apologising to a friend.

Last night you and some friends arranged to meet at a pizza restaurant and then go to the cinema but you couldn't get there. Look at the example and send a message to one of your friends.

• Apologise.
• Give a reason why you did not go.
• Say when you will see them again.

Tony,
I'm really sorry I didn't meet you all at the pizza restaurant last night, but I had to stay at home and look after my younger sister. I'll see you at school on Monday.
Chris

11 > 👀 Listen

Joe has some news for Louise. Listen and choose the best answer.

1 Joe's father wants Joe to phone him about:
   a) the project.
   b) a job for Louise's father.
   c) a problem at home.
2 The company is looking for:
   a) software experts.
   b) people to sell soft toys.
   c) computer salesmen.
3 Louise decides to phone her father:
   a) this evening.
   b) tomorrow.
   c) immediately.

Children of the street

Rob Thompson reports

Eduardo Drio, aged 16, does voluntary work with street children in his home city of Manila, the capital of the Philippines.

'There are over 100 million children in the world who live on the streets because they have no home. I do voluntary work for an organisation which helps street children to get off the streets and to lead a normal life.

There is a big difference between street children and street-working children. Street-working children make money by selling sweets and things. Then they go home. But street children have no home. They live and work on the streets. They sleep on the pavement and in bus shelters. They beg, steal or sell things to make a living.

Here in Manila, our organisation found an area where there were lots of street children. We talked to about sixty of them and gave them food and first aid. Slowly they began to trust us and we persuaded them to come to our hostel to eat and sleep. Most of the kids won't tell us about their backgrounds. But if they want to talk to us about their families and where they come from, we'll listen.

We've also started an education programme. If kids learn a trade, they'll have a chance of finding work. We want them to make something of their lives.'

A boy selling balloons on the streets of Manila

12 > Read

a> Read the text and find phrases which mean the same as the following.

1 unpaid work
2 ask people in the street for money
3 emergency medical help
4 an opportunity of getting a job

b> Read the last two paragraphs and then write these sentences in the correct order.

a) The children regularly went to the hostel at night for food and shelter.
b) They went to class to learn how to do certain jobs.
c) They offered them medical help and something to eat.
d) The organisation chose street children from a certain part of the city.

13 > Over to you

Talk about these questions with a partner.

What voluntary projects do you know about in your country? What sort of voluntary work interests you?

Fast rewind UNITS 16 and 17

Grammar

1 › Match the clauses to make sentences.

1 d) *If you go to the concert early, you'll get good seats.*

1 If you go to the concert early,	a) you'll get spots.
2 You'll get there faster	b) if it's too expensive
3 If you don't leave now,	c) someone will steal it.
4 I won't buy the CD	d) you'll get good seats.
5 If he leaves his bike outside,	e) you'll miss the bus.
6 If you eat too much chocolate,	f) if you go by bike.

2 › Complete the sentences with the correct form of the verbs in brackets.

If it ... very expensive, I ... it. (be; not buy)
If it*'s* very expensive, I *won't buy* it.

1 If he ... some tickets, he ... us to the final. (get; take)
2 If you ... Katie, ... her to phone me? (see; you/ask)
3 We ... be for the film if we ... now. (late; not/leave)
4 The dog ... if you ... the bell. (bark; ring)
5 ... me if there ... any problems? (you/phone; be)
6 He ... ready in time if he ... . (not/be; not/hurry up)

3 › Complete the sentences with *would rather* or *would prefer*.

I*'d prefer* to go swimming.   I*'d rather* go swimming.
1 Which ... you ... to do?
2 They ... go by train.
3 We ... have a disco than a barbecue.
4 She ... to sleep in the small room.
5 Would you like to go out or ... you ... stay in?
6 I ... to telephone her rather than write to her.

Vocabulary

4 › Complete the sentences with the correct word.

We're going to *the beach* today.

1 I'm going ... next weekend.

2 We went ... yesterday afternoon.

3 Would you like to come to ... on Saturday?

4 I've never been ... . Is it difficult?

5 Would you like to come ... with us?

5 › Write the adverb of the word in brackets to complete the sentences.

1	(quick)	I want you to do this *quickly.*
2	(angry)	Why are you looking at me so ...?
3	(early)	I don't like going to bed ... .
4	(late)	She arrived ... for the exams.
5	(slow)	Could you please say it again ... ?
6	(hard)	They tried very ... to win the cup.
7	(good)	He doesn't play tennis very ... .

Communication

6 › Reorder the sentences to complete the conversation.

A: *What shall we do this evening?*

a) So would I. What time does the disco start?
b) Let's go and get ready. It's already seven o'clock.
c) Let's see what's on at the cinema.
d) Well, if you want to do something different, there's a disco at the art college. I'd really like to go.
e) Eight thirty.
f) Oh no, not the cinema. I'd prefer to do something different.

7 › It is your friend's birthday on Sunday. You meet in a café but you are late. Follow the instructions.

A: *Hi, Chris. Sorry I'm late.*

A: Greet your friend and apologise for being late.
B: Accept the apology.
A: Invite B to do something for the evening.
B: Disagree and state your preference.
A: Agree. Ask what presents B hopes to get from his/her family.
B: Reply.
A: Ask what B will buy if he/she gets some money.
B: Reply.

Progress update Units 16 and 17

How do you rate your progress? Tick the chart.

	Excellent ★★★★	Good ★★★	OK ★★	Can do better ★
Grammar				
Vocabulary				
Communication				

18 The scenes are filmed here.

Learning goals

Communication
Remind and reassure people
with *will/won't*

Grammar
The passive: present simple

Vocabulary
Jobs in the media
Types of films

Before you listen

Have you got a favourite TV programme?
What is it?
What questions would you like to ask
the director of a TV soap opera?
Have you ever visited a TV studio?

1> 👀 Listen and read

The group are visiting a TV studio.

Anna: Hello. Welcome everybody. My name's
Anna. I'm your guide this morning.
Please don't forget to wear your security
badges at all times.

Sandra: Don't worry, we won't.

Anna: This is the main studio. Most of the
scenes are filmed here.

Gabriel: Are the episodes made a long time in
advance?

Anna: Yes, they're made about five or six weeks
before they're shown on TV.

Spike: What happens when an actor is ill?

Anna: Well, if someone's ill for a long time, the
storyline's changed.

Louise: Do you ever go abroad to film?

Anna: Yes. Last year we went to France to film
a couple of episodes. Hi, Richard! How
are you?

Spike: *(whispering to Stefan)* He's one of the
actors.

Louise: Go on, Spike! Ask him for his autograph.

Stefan: Remember to smile nicely!

Spike: Shut up, Stefan!

Stefan: Too late! He's gone!

2> Comprehension

Answer the questions.

1 What does Anna remind the group to do?
2 Where does Anna take the group first?
3 What question does the group ask about the
actors?
4 Why was last year different?
5 Who does Anna greet in the studio?
6 What does Louise want Spike to do?

3> 👀 Useful phrases

Listen and repeat.

- How are you?
- Shut up!
- Too late!

4> Vocabulary

Jobs in the media

Match the jobs below with the pictures.

Number 1 is a camera operator.

- actor/actress • director • journalist
- scriptwriter • camera operator
- sound engineer • make-up artist

5> Over to you

Answer the questions.

Would you like to do any of these jobs. Why?

*I'd like to be a camera operator because I'm interested
in photography.*

How a film is made

Grammar snapshot

The passive: present simple
The TV programme **is made** in Liverpool.
The indoor scenes **are filmed** in this studio.

Make a rule.
To make the present simple passive we use the ... tense of the verb *to be* and the ... participle of the main verb.

Go back and look.
Find examples of the present simple passive in the dialogue in Exercise 1.

6 > Practice

Describe how a film is made using the present passive of the verbs in brackets.

1

First an idea for a film (develop)
¹ *is developed* by a film company.
Then a director and a scriptwriter
(employ) ² ... and the script (write) ³ ... .

2

When the producer has found the money to make the film, the actors (choose) ⁴... .

3

Then the sets and costumes (design) ⁵ ... and (make) ⁶ ... . Finally, technicians (employ) ⁷ ... .

4

Film acting is quite difficult because a film script (never film) ⁸ ... in the correct order of events. Actors (often/ask) ⁹ ... to act the same scene many times over.

5

When filming (finish) ¹⁰ ... , the film (put together) ¹¹ ... from thousands of separate shots.

7 Vocabulary Types of films

Can you name a film of each type?

1 'Star Wars' is a science fiction film.

1 science fiction film	5 horror film	9 musical
2 historical film	6 action film	10 comedy
3 gangster film	7 love story	11 cartoon
4 disaster film	8 western	12 thriller

8 Over to you

Think of a film title. In pairs, ask questions to find out the title of your partner's film.

- What sort of film is it? • Who's in it?
- What's it about?

9 ⌁ Listen

Listen to Rupert talking about acting in films and answer the questions.

1 What's the name of his most recent film?
2 What sort of film is it? What's it about?
3 What's his part in it?
4 Where is the film set?
5 What's the boring side of filming?
6 What does Rupert most like about acting in films?

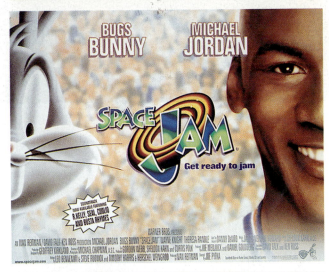

10 ⌁ **Sound**bite

Fall-rise intonation

Don't worry, I won't. (Look at page 123.)

11 Communication

Reminding and reassuring people

▶ Remember to record the film on Channel 4 for me this evening.
▶ Don't worry, I will.
▶ Thanks. And don't forget to switch off the TV when you go to bed.
▶ No, I won't.
▶ And if anyone phones, don't forget to take a message.
▶ No, I won't, I promise.

Your best friend is staying in your home for the weekend. Use the cues to remind him or her to do things while you are away, then add some more instructions.

- record (the film) • switch off (the TV)
- feed (the cat) • take phone messages
- set the alarm

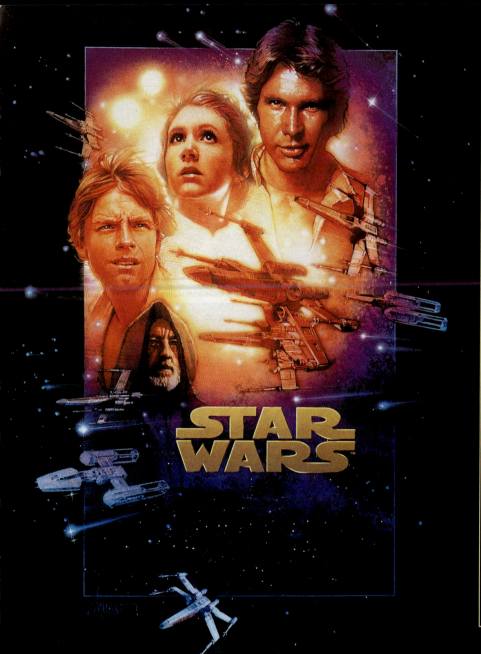

In a galaxy far, far away ...

Star Wars, *The Empire Strikes Back* and *The Return of the Jedi* were record-breaking hit films in the late 70s and early 80s. Recently, director George Lucas restored the films and added some new special effects.

Star Wars is a classic story of good versus evil. The story is set 'a long time ago in a galaxy far, far away'. The galaxy is ruled by the evil Galactic Empire. Luke Skywalker, a young farmboy, lives on the planet of Tatooine with his aunt and uncle. His aunt and uncle are killed. Soon after this, Luke meets Obi-Wan Kenobi, the last of the Jedi knights in the desert. His life is changed forever.

Obi-Wan Kenobi trains Luke to use the powers of the Force to fight the Empire and its leader, the evil Darth Vader.

Luke is joined by two friendly androids, C-3PO and R2-D2. They team up with Han Solo, a mercenary pilot played by Harrison Ford. The group land on Darth Vader's spaceship, the terrifying Death Star, and rescue the beautiful Princess Leia. They escape after an exciting battle and the Death Star is destroyed.

12 > **Help**line

Reading in class.

1 Read the title of the text and use the pictures to help you to predict the content.
2 Keep the reading task in mind while you read.
3 Read in whole phrases, not word by word.
4 Try to guess the meaning of new words from the context.

Now try your reading skills.

Before you read

What type of film is *Star Wars*?
Have you seen the *Star Wars* films?
What are they about?
What are C-3PO and R2-D2?

13 > Read

Read the text and answer the questions.

1 Where is *Star Wars* set?
2 Who is Luke Skywalker?
3 What happens to his aunt and uncle?
4 What is Luke trained to do?
5 Who is rescued from the Death Star?
6 What happens at the end?

14 > Write

Write a paragraph about a film which you have seen recently and enjoyed.

Last week I saw 'Titanic'. It's a disaster film directed by James Cameron. It's set in 1912 on the ship the Titanic. The ship hits an iceberg and most of the passengers are drowned. The main stars are Leonardo DiCaprio and Kate Winslet. It's a really good film.

A party

Read the story and try to guess the missing words. Then listen and see if you were right.

I really enjoyed the visit to the TV studios today.
Yes, it was great. Mick wasn't there!

____ Mick this morning? What's he done wrong?
I wanted to have a party. And Mick said no!

Let's ____ this evening anyway!
Good idea.
Don't forget to bring your guitar.
Don't worry, I won't.

____ glasses!
I think they're kept in here.

____ in my room! Now!
Great! I'll bring some of my cassettes.

Let's dance!
No, ____ .
It doesn't matter if we make a noise. We're all going home soon.

What on earth is going on?

109

Learning goals

Communication
Order food and drink in a restaurant

Grammar
The passive: past simple
much, many, a lot of

Vocabulary
Food and drink in a restaurant

1 › **Read**

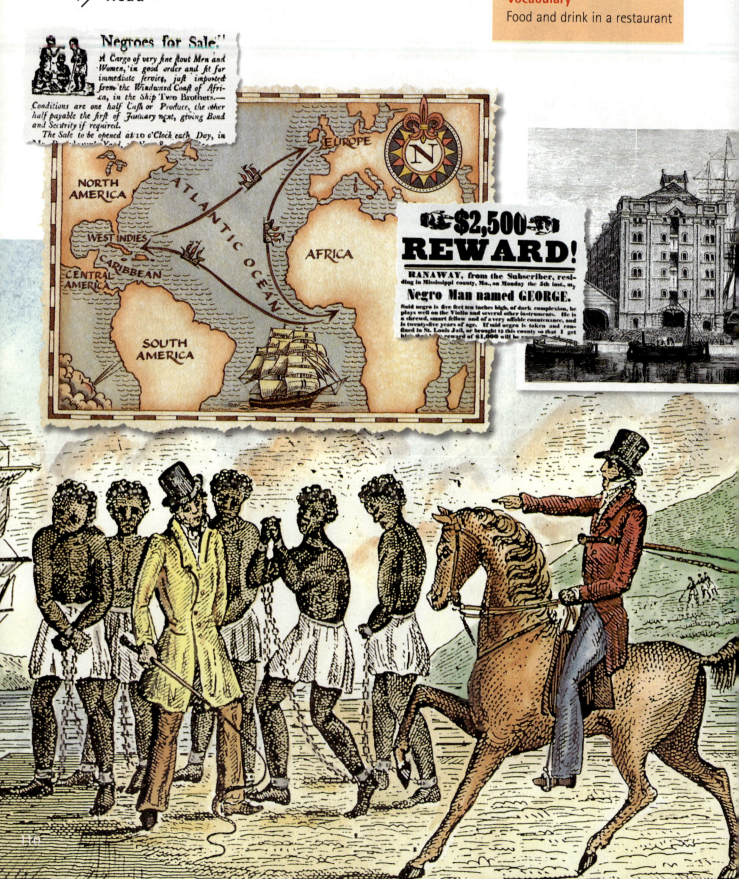

Negroes for Sale.

A Cargo of very fine stout Men and Women, in good order and fit for immediate service, just imported from the Windward Coast of Africa, in the Ship Two Brothers.—

Conditions are one half Cash or Produce, the other half payable the first of January next, giving Bond and Security if required.

The Sale to be opened at 10 o'Clock each Day, in

$2,500 REWARD!

RANAWAY, from the Subscriber, residing in Mississippi county, Mo., on Monday the 5th inst., m, **Negro Man named GEORGE.**

Said negro is five feet ten inches high, of dark complexion, he plays well on the Violin and several other instruments. He is a shrewd, smart fellow and of a very affable countenance, and is twenty-five years of age. If said negro is taken and confined in St. Louis Jail, or brought to this county so that I get him, then the reward of $1,000 will be ...

The transatlantic slave trade

The main European nations who were involved in the transatlantic slave trade were Britain, France, Portugal, Spain, Holland, Denmark and Sweden. From about 1730 to 1800 Liverpool was the most important port.

The transatlantic slave trade usually followed a triangular route. Traders left the European ports and went to the west coast of Africa. In exchange for goods like alcohol, cloth and guns, they bought African people and put them onto their ships. These future slaves were taken across the Atlantic to the Americas and the West Indies. The voyage took six to eight weeks.

Liverpool Docks

Conditions on board the slave ships were terrible. The men were kept together below deck. There wasn't much room so they were forced to lie down. The women and children were separated from the men. In good weather the slaves were brought on deck and forced to exercise. They were fed twice a day. A lot of people were sick and died of disease during the voyage. Those who died were thrown overboard.

When they reached their destination, the Africans were sold as slaves. The traders used the money to buy cheap local products such as sugar, rum, coffee, tobacco, rice and cotton, which were then taken back to Europe and sold. The slave traders made a lot of money at every point of the triangle.

Almost half of the slaves were taken to the Caribbean. Large numbers were also taken to Central and South America. About one in twenty were taken to the southern states of North America. They were forced by their owners to learn a new language and new customs and to work for nothing. A lot of slaves died or committed suicide.

The slave trade was abolished in Britain in 1807.

2 Comprehension

a Complete the notes.

The transatlantic slave trade	
European countries involved:	......
Period of Liverpool's importance:	......
The triangular trade route:	......
Destinations of the slaves:	......

b Write questions for these answers.

1 How long was the voyage across the Atlantic?

1 Six to eight weeks.
2 Twice a day.
3 Sugar, rum, coffee and other local products.
4 In 1807.

c Find words in the text which mean the same as the following.

1 journey across the sea
2 extremely bad
3 divided
4 serious illness
5 killed themselves
6 stopped and made illegal

3 ⊡ Listen

Listen to Liz and Chris talking about a visit to the Museum of Slavery in Liverpool and answer the questions.

1 Why was Liz horrified?
2 What surprised Chris?
3 What was Liz shown at the end of their visit?

4 Over to you

Answer the questions.

What have been the results of the slave trade?
Are there places in the world where slavery still exists? If so, what can we do to stop it?

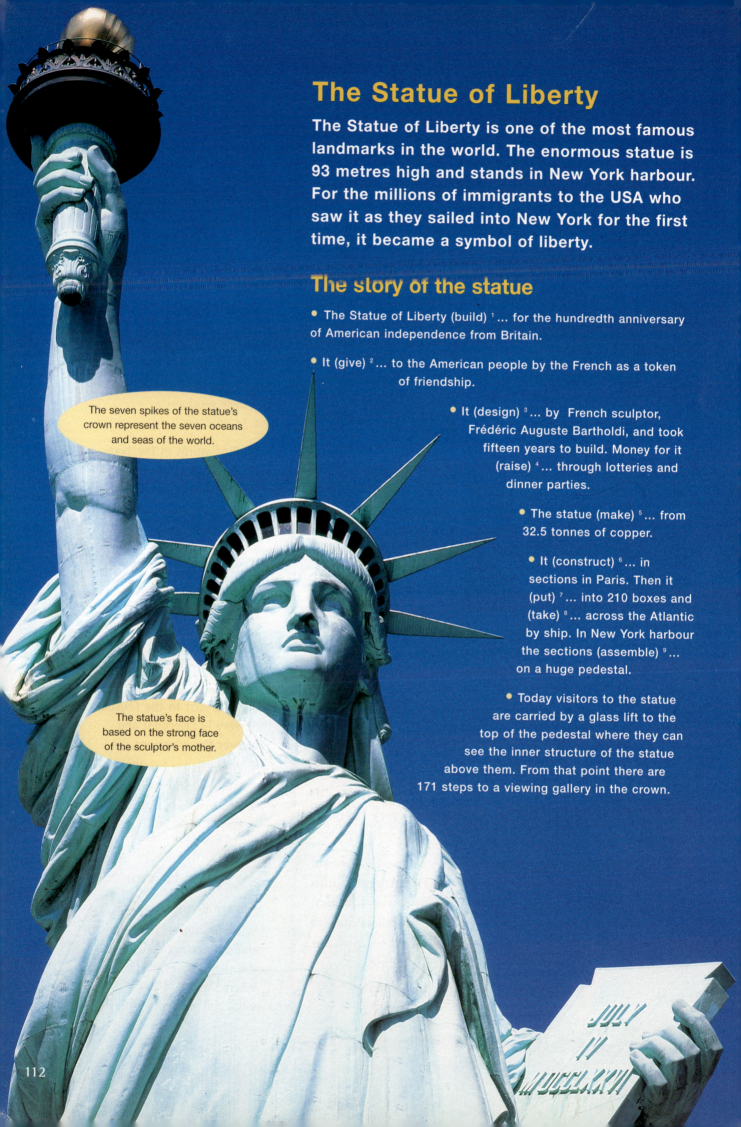

The Statue of Liberty

The Statue of Liberty is one of the most famous landmarks in the world. The enormous statue is 93 metres high and stands in New York harbour. For the millions of immigrants to the USA who saw it as they sailed into New York for the first time, it became a symbol of liberty.

The story of the statue

- The Statue of Liberty (build) [1] ... for the hundredth anniversary of American independence from Britain.

- It (give) [2] ... to the American people by the French as a token of friendship.

- It (design) [3] ... by French sculptor, Frédéric Auguste Bartholdi, and took fifteen years to build. Money for it (raise) [4] ... through lotteries and dinner parties.

- The statue (make) [5] ... from 32.5 tonnes of copper.

- It (construct) [6] ... in sections in Paris. Then it (put) [7] ... into 210 boxes and (take) [8] ... across the Atlantic by ship. In New York harbour the sections (assemble) [9] ... on a huge pedestal.

- Today visitors to the statue are carried by a glass lift to the top of the pedestal where they can see the inner structure of the statue above them. From that point there are 171 steps to a viewing gallery in the crown.

The seven spikes of the statue's crown represent the seven oceans and seas of the world.

The statue's face is based on the strong face of the sculptor's mother.

Grammar snapshot

The passive: past simple
The slave trade **was abolished** in 1807.
Many slaves **were taken** to the West Indies.

Make a rule.
To make the past simple passive we use the ... tense of the verb
... and the ... participle of the main verb.

5〉 Practice

**a〉 Read about the Statue of Liberty and use the past passive
form of the verb in brackets to complete the information.**

**b〉 In pairs, use the cues to make questions about the Statue
of Liberty. Then ask and answer them.**

A: *Why was the Statue of Liberty given to the people of the USA?*
B: *It was given by the people of France as a token of friendship.*

1 Why/the Statue of Liberty/give to/the people of the USA?
2 What/it/build for?
3 Who/statue/design by?
4 What/the statue/make of?
5 How/it/take/across the Atlantic?

6〉 😎 Soundbite The sound / ə / (schwa)

was (used)   were (taken)   (Look at page 123.)

The neutral vowel in unstressed syllables and weak forms is
the most common vowel sound in English.

7〉 Interaction

Student B: Turn to page 121.

Student A: Use one of the verbs below to complete the quiz
questions. Then ask Student B the questions.

A: *Where was the Statue of Liberty designed?*
B: *It was designed in France.*

• assassinate • build • design • write • invent

1 Where ... the Statue of Liberty ...?
2 When ... the Pyramids ...?
3 When ... the Morse Code ...?
4 Who ... *Oliver Twist* ... by?
5 Where ... Abraham Lincoln ...?

Now choose the correct answer for Student B's questions.

• By a volcanic eruption. • Beethoven. • In 1869.
• Picasso. • In 1927.

Grammar flash

much, many, a lot of

Positive statements
There was **a lot of** room.
There were **a lot of** men.
A lot of people died.

Negative statements
There was**n't much** room.
There were**n't many** women and
  children.
Not many people survived.

Questions
Was there **much** water?
Were there **many** children?

**Make rules about countable and
uncountable nouns.**
1 We use *much* with ... nouns.
2 We use *many* with ... nouns.
3 *A lot of* can be used with both ... and
  ... nouns.

Notes
1 We generally use *much* and *many* in
  negative statements and questions.
2 We never use *much* in positive
  statements.

8〉 Practice

Complete the sentences with *much,
many* **or** *a lot of.*

1 Let's hurry. We haven't got ... time.
2 How ... tickets do you need?
3 Do you have ... trouble with
  pronunciation?
4 Are there ... cinemas in your town?
5 There was ... noise at the party.
6 There weren't ... students in class
  today.
7 ... money was made in Liverpool
  from the slave trade.

~ WELCOME TO ~

WORLD FAMOUS

Barry Marsden's

FISH AND CHIP RESTAURANT

Try Barry's Special

Fish, chips, peas or beans, bread and butter and a choice of tea, coffee or a soft drink

£3.25

~Starters~

Soup £1.20

Orange juice or Tomato juice £1

~Main courses~

Fish or fish cakes £2.00

Scampi £2.20

Roast beef £3.00

Hamburger £1.95

Vegeburger £1.95

Side orders

Green salad £1.50

Chips £1.00

Peas £1.25

Beans £1.25

~Sweets~

Apple pie £1.75

Ice cream (chocolate, vanilla or strawberry) £1.50

~Drinks~

Coke 80p

Sparkling mineral water 90p

Lemonade 80p

Tea 60p

Coffee 75p

Milk 65p

9 ⊙⊙ Listen

Listen to the group ordering a meal at Barry Marsden's. Say whether the sentences are T (true), F (false) or DK (don't know).

1 The fish and chip restaurant is famous.

2 The group have got a lot of time left in Liverpool.

3 Fish and chips is an unusual meal to have in Britain.

4 Louise has a diet coke and Sandra orders a sparkling mineral water.

5 Everyone has the same dish.

6 Barry's Special is the cheapest dish on the menu.

7 Everyone is going to pay separately for his/her meal.

10 Communication

Ordering food and drink in a restaurant

▶ What would you like to start with?

▷ Can I have the soup, please?

▶ And to follow?

▷ I'll have the fish cakes, please.

▶ Any side orders?

▷ Yes. Chips, please.

▶ Would you like a sweet?

▷ No, thank you. That's fine.

▶ What about something to drink?

▷ Can I have a diet coke, please?

In groups, order a meal from the menu.

11 **Help**line

English outside the classroom.

Here are some things you can do to improve your English.

1 Look out for English words in shops, in the street, and on menus in cafés and restaurants.

2 Buy British or American magazines or comics.

3 Speak to tourists if you have an opportunity.

4 Write down the words of English or American pop songs.

5 Watch video films which have subtitles and are not dubbed.

6 Use the Internet if you have the opportunity.

Fast rewind UNITS 18 and 19

Grammar

1> Complete the sentences with a present or past passive of the verb in brackets.

Jaws by Steven Spielberg (direct)
'Jaws' was directed by Steven Spielberg.

1 Tea ... in Sri Lanka. (grow)
2 Our flats ... in the 1980s. (build)
3 Their school exams ... always ... in June. (hold)
4 ... your cousin... during the match? (hurt)
5 The men... two days after the robbery. (catch)
6 His wallet... when he was in the market. (steal)
7 ... your computer ... to the Internet now? (connect)

2> Write sentences with *there was/there were* **and** *much/many/a lot of.*

(✓) noise in the street last night.
There was a lot of noise in the street last night.

1 (✓) ... really good films on TV last week.
2 (✗) ... people at Anna's party.
3 (?) ... good exhibitions in Liverpool last year?
4 (?) ... money in the wallet?
5 (✗) ... food left after the barbecue.
6 (✓) ... things to do in the evening.
7 (✗) ... time to go sightseeing.
8 (✓) ... thousands of people at the pop concert.

3> Correct the underlined verb phrases in these sentences.

We <u>work</u> on a project in Liverpool at the moment.
We are working on a project in Liverpool at the moment.

1 <u>I'm like</u> modern ballet.
2 This watch <u>was make</u> in Switzerland.
3 <u>Have you gone</u> to the cinema last night?
4 <u>She worked</u> in the garden when I met her.
5 <u>My parents was</u> in London three times before.
6 <u>I phone</u> you tomorrow if I have time.
7 If it <u>will rain</u>, we'll go to the museum.
8 Why <u>not we have</u> a rock 'n' roll party?

4> Write the short form answers.

Are you English? (No) *No, I'm not.*

1 Can you speak Russian? (No)
2 Have you got a lot of money with you? (Yes)
3 Do they live in London? (Yes)
4 Does your sister like going to parties? (No)
5 Will it be cold in Spain in November? (No)
6 Have you both finished your homework? (No)
7 Should I get a new computer? (Yes)

Vocabulary

5> Complete the definitions.

A person who writes for a newspaper is a *journalist*.

A person who:
1 acts in plays is an ... .
2 directs a play is a ... .
3 records the sound for a film is a ... .
4 writes a film script is a ... .
5 operates a camera is a ... .
6 changes an actor's appearance is a ... .

Communication

6> Reorder the sentences to complete the conversation in a restaurant.

A: *What would you like to start with?*

a) And to follow?
b) What would you like with your fish?
c) Can I have soup to start with, please?
d) Chips, please.
e) I'll have the fish, please.
f) Can I have a diet coke, please?
g) No, thank you. That's fine.
h) OK. Chips. And a green salad?
i) What about something to drink?

6> Work in pairs. Student A:
Ask Student B
• what food products your country is known for.
• where they are produced or grown.
• when your school was built.

Now Student B:
Ask Student A
• where he/she thinks the best cars are made.
• where the best sports clothes are sold in your area.
• when a famous building in your country was built.

Progress update Units 18 and 19

How do you rate your progress? Tick the chart.

	Excellent ★★★★	Good ★★★	OK ★★	Can do better ★
Grammar				
Vocabulary				
Communication				

A diary of hope

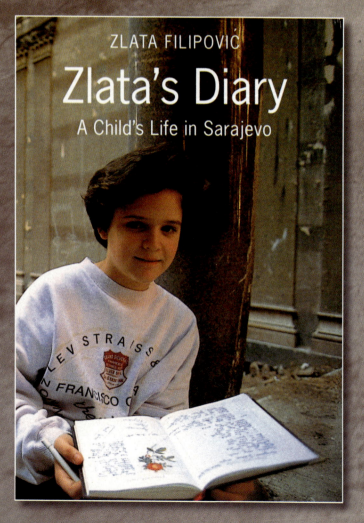

ZLATA FILIPOVIC

Zlata's Diary
A Child's Life in Sarajevo

In September 1991, in the city of Sarajevo in Bosnia, a young girl started to write a diary. Then a war began. For two years, while people were fighting each other and her city was bombed and shelled, Zlata Filipovic wrote her thoughts in her diary. Later the diary was published by Unicef. It is called *Zlata's Diary: A Child's Life in Sarajevo*.

Before the war, Zlata's life was very pleasant. She lived with her family in a big, comfortable apartment in Sarajevo. She was given everything she wanted – piano lessons, tennis lessons, weekends in the country and holidays in Italy.

In the beginning, Zlata wrote in her diary about all the things a typical teenager is interested in – pop stars, super models, school grades and skiing trips. Then the war started. For the next two years Zlata wrote about the war in Bosnia. Her parents were nervous all the time, and her mother cried regularly.

On the outside, Zlata remained calm, but on the inside she was very angry. She wrote about her anger in her diary: she called the politicians 'kids'. Like children, they were playing games – not with toys, but with people's lives.

"They have stolen something from us. They have taken away our childhood." When her school was shut down, she wrote: "I've lost the most precious thing in my life."

Zlata's diary is remarkable because it gives a young person's view of war. Everyday life is described in detail: how they ran to the cellar when the shelling started; how they quickly used the washing machine when the electricity came on for a few hours; how they bathed carefully using jugs of water and plastic sheets.

But Zlata and her family still tried to have normal lives. They celebrated birthdays. Zlata read books and she played games. She practised the piano. She even took a music exam and passed it.

Now the war in Bosnia is finished, Zlata and her family have begun a new life in Dublin in Ireland. Zlata will go back to Sarajevo if the peace lasts. "I sincerely hope the peace will last, because Sarajevo is where my heart is."

Before you read

What do you know about the war in Bosnia?

1 〉 Read

a) Read about Zlata and guess the meaning of these words. Check your answers with your teacher or dictionary.

- war
- fight (*v.*)
- nervous
- regularly
- calm
- precious
- jug
- plastic sheet
- peace

b) Read the text again and put the topics in the correct order.

1 *b) Zlata's life at home before the war.*
a) Zlata's life after the war.
b) Zlata's life at home before the war.
c) The start of the war.
d) How her family tried to lead a normal life.
e) Her anger at the politicians.
f) Her life at home during the war.

2 〉 Speak

Talk about changes in your life and in the lives of members of your family in the past three years.

3 〉 ⟨••⟩ Listen

Listen to a scriptwriter talking about his diary. Note his answers to these questions.

1 How long has he kept a diary?
2 What sort of things did he write as a teenager?
3 How often does he write in his diary?
4 Why does he keep a diary today?
5 In his story, what did the old lady write on the piece of paper?
6 What did he think it meant? What *did* it mean?

4 〉 Write

Write a diary entry for a lucky/unlucky day. Say what happened and how you felt.

Project ▶ ④ *Snapshot of a famous place*

Write a project about a famous monument, building or place in your country and find pictures to illustrate it.

Stonehenge, Britain

Where is it situated? When was it built?

Stonehenge is Britain's most famous monument. It is a group of enormous stones situated on Salisbury Plain in the south of England. It was built between 2000 B.C. and 1400 B.C. and many of the original stones are still standing today.

What does it look like?

There are two main circles of stones, one inside the other. In the centre the stones are in a horseshoe shape around a central block. The whole monument is surrounded by a ditch.

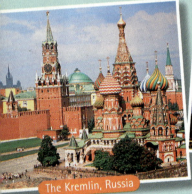
The Kremlin, Russia

The Colosseum, Italy

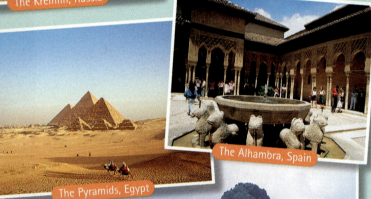
The Pyramids, Egypt

The Alhambra, Spain

Machu Picchu, Peru

How was it built?

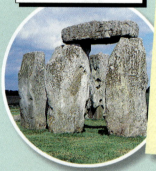

Some of the stones weigh 50 tonnes. They were brought to the area from a distance of 30 kilometres. The stones were then shaped before they were erected.

Why was it built?

No one is sure why Stonehenge was built. Some people say it was used as a temple to worship the sun and that the block in the centre was an altar. But archaeologists now think that it was an astronomical observatory to study the movements of the sun, moon and stars.

Thanks for everything!

Read the story and try to guess the missing sentences. Then listen and see if you were right.

1. Where's Spike?

_____ . She was standing here a few minutes ago.

2. Sandra, if I send you an e-mail, _____ ?

Don't be silly, Sam!

Yes, of course I will.

3. Goodbye, Mr Brennan. _____ .

Oh, you mean the party? Don't worry. I'm a light sleeper.

4. The London train is leaving in a couple of minutes.

Are you coming with us, Joe?

No, my father's coming from Manchester to pick me up.

5. _____ .

Next week? No, phone me tonight!

6. Cheers, Gabriel! Have a good trip. _____ Spain, I'll visit you.

That would be great.

7. Come on Spike! The train's just leaving. Hurry up!

Or do you want to stay here and work for another week?

No, thanks! Bye!

8. Bye, everyone!

Bye! Thanks for everything!

119

Take a break

She's leaving home

This song was written by John Lennon and Paul McCartney. It comes from one of the Beatles' most innovative albums, *Sergeant Pepper's Lonely Hearts Club Band*, which was released in 1967. Of all the Beatles' songs, *She's leaving home* is one of the most moving. It tells the sad story of a family breaking up and seems to symbolise the bitter relationships that can exist between parents and children.

Wednesday morning at five o'clock as the day begins,
Silently closing the bedroom [1] ....
Leaving the note that she hoped would say more,
She goes downstairs to the kitchen
Clutching her handkerchief,
Quietly turning the backdoor key,
Stepping outside she is [2] ....
She *(We gave her most of our lives)*
is leaving *(Sacrificed most of our lives)*
home. *(We gave her everything money could buy)*
She's leaving home after living alone
For so many years. *(Bye, bye)*

Father snores as his wife gets into her dressing gown,
Picks up the letter that's lying [3] ....
Standing alone at the top of the stairs,
She breaks down and cries to her husband,
"Daddy, our baby's gone!
Why would she treat us so thoughtlessly?
How could she do this to [4] ....?"
She *(We never thought of ourselves)*
is leaving *(Never a thought for ourselves)*
home. *(We struggled hard all our lives to get by)*
She's leaving home after living alone
For so many years. *(Bye, bye)*

Friday morning at nine o'clock she is far away,
Waiting to keep an appointment she [5] .... ,
Meeting a man from the motor trade.
She *(What did we do that was wrong?)*
is having *(We didn't know it was wrong)*
fun. *(Fun is the one thing that money can't buy)*
One thing inside that was always denied
For so many years. *(Bye, bye)*
She's leaving home. Bye, bye.

1> 👀 Read the lyrics of the song and guess which of these words fits each gap. Then listen and see if you were right.
- made   • there   • door   • me   • free

2> Guess the meaning of these words and phrases from the song.
- clutching   • sacrificed   • to snore
- dressing gown   • to break down
- to struggle   • motor trade   • to deny

3> Answer the questions.
1 What has happened?
2 How do her parents feel?

4> Think about it.
1 How old do you think the girl is?
2 Why is she leaving home?
3 How do you think she feels?

Student B section

Unit 4 4> Interaction

Student B: Use the checklist of things you've got in the kitchen to answer Student A's questions.

Checklist

In kitchen	Not in kitchen
Butter	Eggs
Oil	Cheese
Salt and pepper	Vinegar
Lettuce	Tomatoes
	Cucumber

Unit 8 5> Interaction

Student B: First use the information in your factfile to answer Student A's questions about Harrison Ford. Then ask Student A questions to complete your information.

B: *What were Harrison Ford's parents called?*

A: *They were called Christopher and Dorothy.*

B: *What happened/What did he do when he was 12?*

A: *He ...*

He's Han Solo and Indiana Jones. He's the star of many Hollywood blockbusters. His name is **Harrison Ford**.

Born: On July 13 1942 in Chicago, Illinois, USA

Parents: ......

First hobby: Keeps rats

Aged 12: ......

Aged 18: Goes to Ripon College, Wisconsin to study philosophy

Outside college: ......

Aged 22: Joins Williams Bay Theater Group and gets married

Aged 24: ......

Aged 30: Makes two more films, including *American Graffiti*

Job: ......

Aged 34: Gets his big break as Han Solo in *Star Wars*

Some other important films: *The Empire Strikes Back, Raiders of the Lost Ark, Blade Runner, Witness, Working Girl, The Fugitive, The Devil's Own, Air Force One*

Unit 14 7> Interaction

Student B: Use the information below to answer Student A's questions about Rory and Jenny. Then find out from Student A about the jobs Tanya and Ray are doing on work experience and complete the chart.

B: *Where is Tanya doing work experience?*

A: *In a children's play group.*

B: *What does she have to do?*

A: ...

B: *Does she have to wear a uniform?*

A: ...

B: *What time does she have to start?*

A: ...

Name	Tanya Lane	Rory Grant	Ray Sharman	Jenny Trim
Job	?	At a hospital	?	In an office
Duties	?	Serving tea and coffee Making beds	?	Answering the phone Stamping letters and taking them to the post office
Uniform	?	White nylon	?	Jacket, blouse and dark skirt
Hours	?	7.30–3.30	?	9.00–5.00

Unit 19 7> Interaction

Student B: Choose the correct answer for Student A's questions.

A: *Where was the Statue of Liberty designed?*

B: *It was designed in France.*

- Charles Dickens
- In France.
- In a theatre.
- Between 2000 and 1000 BC.
- In 1838.

Now use one of the verbs below to complete the quiz questions. Then ask Student A the questions.

- destroy • paint • compose • make • open

1 When ... the first solo flight across the Atlantic ...?
2 When ... the Suez Canal ...?
3 How ... Pompeii ...?
4 Who ... *Guernica* ... by?
5 Who ... the *1912 Overture* ... by?

Soundbite exercises

Unit 1   9> •• Soundbite

The sounds / sp /, / st / and / sk /   Spike   Stella   school

a> Listen and repeat.

/ sp / **Sp**ike   / st / **St**ella   / sk / **sch**ool
This is **Sp**ike and that's **St**ella.
Gabriel's a **st**udent from **Sp**ain.

b> Now listen and repeat the sentences.

Spike is at the **st**ation
He likes **sk**iing and **sk**ating.
Some English **st**udents **st**udy **Sp**anish at **sch**ool.

Unit 2   3> •• Soundbite

Sentence stress   It's <u>on</u> the <u>floor</u>.   It's <u>under</u> the <u>desk</u>.

**Listen to the sentences and mark the stressed words or
syllables.**

It's <u>on</u> the <u>floor</u>. It's <u>on</u> the <u>bed</u>. It's <u>in</u> the <u>box</u>.
It's <u>on</u> the <u>table</u>.
It's <u>under</u> the <u>desk</u>. It's <u>next</u> to the <u>bed</u>. It's <u>under</u> the <u>bed</u>.
It's be<u>hind</u> the <u>bed</u>. It's a<u>bove</u> the <u>desk</u>.
It's in <u>front</u> of the <u>door</u>. It's in <u>front</u> of the <u>house</u>.

b> Listen again and repeat the sentences.

Unit 3   6> •• Soundbite

The sounds / ps /, / ts / and / ks /   shops   starts   talks

a> Listen and repeat.

/ ps /   sho**ps**   sto**ps**   ho**pes**   dro**ps**
/ ts /   star**ts**   visi**ts**   wai**ts**   ha**tes**   no**tes**
/ ks /   tal**ks**   wor**ks**   wal**ks**   li**kes**   ma**kes**   ta**kes**

b> Now listen and repeat the sentences.

She sho**ps** and sho**ps** until she dro**ps**!
He pain**ts** ca**ts**, boa**ts** and ha**ts**.
Sally sa**ys** she li**kes** chocola**tes**, cris**ps** and ca**kes**.
But Sharon sa**ys** she li**kes** swee**ts** and nu**ts**.

Unit 4   9> •• Soundbite

The sounds / tʃ / and / dʒ /   cheese   chips   juice   jam

a> Listen and repeat.

/ tʃ /   **ch**eese   **ch**ocolate   **ch**ips   **ch**icken   **Ch**ina   sandwi**ch**
/ dʒ /   **j**uice   **j**ust   **j**am   **J**anuary   **J**ill   oran**g**e

b> Now listen and repeat the sentences.

John wants a **ch**eese sandwi**ch** and an oran**g**e **j**uice for lun**ch**.
The **ch**ildren have **j**am sandwi**ch**es and oran**g**e **j**uice after
s**ch**ool.
Shelley usually **ch**ooses **ch**ocolate **ch**ip ice cream.

Unit 6   10> •• Soundbite

The sound / θ /   third   eighth   ninth

a> Listen and repeat.

/ θ /   **th**ird   eigh**th**   nin**th**
October the nin**th**
July the four**th**

b> Now listen and repeat the sentences.

I was born on January the fifteen**th** 1987.
It's his sixteen**th** bir**th**day this **Th**ursday.
Theo and **Th**elma are bo**th** thirteen on **Th**ursday.

Unit 7   2> •• Soundbite

The sounds / t /, / d / and / ɪd /
stopped   listened   wanted

a> Listen and repeat.

/ t /   stopp**ed**   watch**ed**   lik**ed**   talk**ed**
/ d /   listen**ed**   rain**ed**   stay**ed**   play**ed**
/ ɪd /   want**ed**   hat**ed**   start**ed**   visit**ed**

b> Now listen to the verbs in these sentences.
      Which ending can you hear: / t /, / d / or / ɪd /?

1 She liked the book.
2 He stopped the car.
3 They hated the film.
4 It rained all day.
5 We wanted to go home.
6 They played a match.
7 The class started late.

c> Listen again and repeat the sentences.

Unit 9   4> •• Soundbite

The sounds / ɔː / and / ɒ /   horse   fox

a> Listen and repeat.

/ ɔː /   h**or**se   s**aw**   m**or**e   of c**our**se   f**our**   w**or**e
/ ɒ /   f**o**x   h**o**t   g**o**t   n**o**t   T**o**m   wh**a**t   sh**o**p

b> Now listen and repeat the sentences.

We s**aw** f**our** white h**or**ses.
Oh, wh**a**t a l**o**t of p**o**pcorn you've g**o**t.
They haven't g**o**t wh**a**t I want in the sh**o**p.

Unit 11   6> •• Soundbite

The sound / h /   have   haven't

a> Listen and repeat.

/ h /   **h**ave   **h**aven't   **h**as   **h**asn't
      how   **wh**o   **h**eard   **h**it   **h**ope

b> Now listen and repeat the sentences.

How many **h**orses **h**as **H**arry got?
I **h**aven't **h**ad a letter from **h**im. **H**ave you?
Have you **h**ad a **h**oliday in **H**avana?
They **h**aven't **h**ad a **h**it single for a year.

Unit 12 6> (••) Sound**bite**

Sentence stress   It's the <u>long</u>est <u>ride</u> in the <u>world</u>.

Listen and repeat the sentences. Make sure you stress the important words and syllables.

It's the longest ride in the world.
He's the cleverest boy in the school.
It's the fastest car in the world.
It's the most beautiful place on earth.
It's the most interesting film this year.

Unit 13 6> (••) Sound**bite**

The sound / l /   I'll he'll

a> **Listen and repeat.**

/ l /   I'll he'll she'll it'll we'll you'll they'll

b> **Now listen and repeat the sentences.**

I'll be fifteen tomorrow.
He'll phone her tomorrow.
We'll ask her to lunch.
They'll be twenty minutes late.
You'll feel better soon.

c> **Say these pairs of sentences. Then listen and check your pronunciation.**

I see her every day.   I'll see her every day.
We have lunch at two.   We'll have lunch at two.
They arrive after breakfast. They'll arrive after breakfast.

Unit 14 10> (••) Sound**bite**

Word stress   <u>doc</u>tor beau<u>ti</u>cian

a> **Listen and repeat. Put the stress on the first syllable of each word.**

<u>doc</u>tor <u>plum</u>ber <u>wai</u>ter <u>den</u>tist <u>clea</u>ner <u>sec</u>retary <u>car</u>penter

b> **Listen and repeat. Put the stress on the second syllable of each word.**

beau<u>ti</u>cian re<u>cep</u>tionist as<u>sis</u>tant

c> **Now listen and repeat the sentences.**

We need a plumber and a carpenter.
I'd like to be a doctor and my sister would like to be a dentist.
My brother's a hotel receptionist.
I'd like to be a hairdresser or a beautician.

Unit 16 6> (••) Sound**bite**

I like /aɪˈlaɪk/ and I'd like /aɪdˈlaɪk/

I like your jacket. **I'd like** your jacket.

a> **Listen and say which sound you hear each time:**

Sound 1 *like* **or Sound 2** *'d like* **(the short form of** *would like***).**

a)   b)   c)   d)   e)   f)

a) I'd like to go to the cinema.   Answers
Sound 2
b) I like your bike.   Sound 1
c) They like classical music.   Sound 1
d) We'd like a coffee, please.   Sound 2
e) We like your flat.   Sound 1
f) They'd like to see the exhibition. Sound 2

b> **Listen again and repeat the sentences.**

I'd like to go to the cinema.
I like your bike.
They like classical music.
We'd like a coffee, please.
We like your flat.
They'd like to see the exhibition.

Unit 17 7> (••) Sound**bite**

Intonation in conditional sentences

If you go now, you'll have lots of time.

a> **Listen and repeat.**

If you go now, ...
If I go out, ...
If I see Joe, ...
If we don't book now, ...

b> **Now listen and repeat the sentences.**

If you go now, you'll have lots of time.
If I go out, Linda will probably phone.
If I see Joe, I'll give him your phone number.
If we don't book now, we won't get any tickets.

Unit 18 10> (••) Sound**bite**

Fall-rise intonation   Don't worry, I won't.

Listen and repeat.

Don't worry, I won't.
I won't, I promise.
Never mind, it's OK.
I'll do it, it's all right.
I will, don't worry.

Unit 19 6> (••) Sound**bite**

The sound / ə /   was were

The neutral vowel in unstressed syllables and weak forms is the most common vowel sound in English

a> **Listen and repeat.**

/ ə /   was used were taken

b> **Now listen and repeat the sentences.**

It was closed.
They were closed.
When was it built?
When was it abolished?
Where were they made?
Where were they taken?

Vocabulary and expressions

Unit 1

Countries and nationalities
Argentina/
  Argentinian
Brazil/
  Brazilian
Britain/British
England/English
France/French
Germany/German
Greece/Greek
Italy/Italian
Jamaica/
  Jamaican
Poland/Polish
Portugal/
  Portuguese
Scandinavia/
  Scandinavian
Spain/Spanish
Turkey/Turkish
UK/British
USA/American

Family members

Types of music
classical
country and
  western
guitar music
heavy metal
jazz
pop
rap
reggae
soul
techno

accommodation
across
area
around (= about)
Art
attraction
August
boat
centre
century
check
cinema
city
club
commercial
community
Computer science
concert hall
contain
cotton
cultural
dock
during
emigrant

everybody/everyone
exciting
exhibition
ferry
first-class
flat
food
free
gallery
group
History
holidays
hostel
industrial
interested (in)
interesting
large
late
leader
Let's go!
lively
location
look at
main
maritime
meet
million
museum
near
north(-west)
of course
organise
other(s)
outside
party
pay (n.)
people
photo
Physics
popular
population
port
project (n.)
real
really
restaurant
river
sea
slaves
Sorry
sort (n.)
spell
story
subject (school
  subject)
suburbs
sugar
summer
superb
surname
take
teenager
theatre

tobacco
tourist
trade
trip
turn down (music)
university
view
visit (v.)
volunteer
warden
welcome

Unit 2

Parts of a room, furniture and objects
armchair
bed
bookcase
carpet
chair
cupboard
curtain
desk
door
duvet
floor
lamp
mirror
noticeboard
picture
poster
radiator
radio
sofa
table
TV
vase
wall
wardrobe
washbasin
wastepaper bin
window

Colours
beige
black
blue
brown
green
grey
pink
purple
red
white
yellow

Patterns
checked
patterned
plain
spotted
striped

Prepositions of place
above
behind
between
in
in front of
in the corner
next to
on the left/right (of)
opposite
under

afraid (I'm afraid)
basic
bit (a bit)
bring
by (= before)
calculator
chew
collect
dictionary
drawing pin
exam
forget
front door
guest
gum
Hey!
homework
jewellery
keep
key
know
leave
light (opp. heavy)
make-up
Maths
mobile phone
move around
office
pale
personal stereo
phone call
polite
present (n.)
public (adj.)
put
share
snack
sound system
stairs
stay out
time (on time)
uncle
use
wear

Unit 3

Clock times

Free-time activities

accident
act (v.)
actor
afternoon
airport
always
best (at my best)
big(gest)
breakfast
common room
depend
diet (v.)
disco
distance
early
eat
excited
Excuse me
fair
feel
few
finish
first thing
football match
get up
gig
give (an interview)
golf
Good!
gym
high (on a high)
How often?
important
Internet
join
junk (food)
keep fit
last (v.)
lead singer
letter
look for
lunch (break)
member
minibus
moment (at the ...)
mood (in the ...)
morning
myself
need
never
often
once
only
opera
ordinary
plane
play (v.)
prefer
relax
relatives
rent (v.)
rock band
routine

run
sell
show (n.)
Shut up!
sing
sleep
sometimes
stage
stay
still
straight (adv.)
study
surf (v.)
swim
time
times (three times)
tired
today
tour (on tour)
travel
twice
until
usually
video (game)
watch (v.)
week
weightlifting
What's the matter?
win
write
youth centre

Unit 4

Food and drink
apple
banana
beans
beef
biscuit
bread
butter
cake
carbohydrate
carrot
cheese
chicken
chips
cucumber
dairy product
doughnut
egg
fat
fish
fruit
hamburger
lamb
lemon
lettuce
meat
melon
milk
muesli

mushroom
nuts
olive oil
omelette
onion
orange
pasta
peach
peas
pepper
pizza
potato
protein
rice
salad
salt
sandwich
sauce
spaghetti
sugar
tomato
tuna
vegetable
vinegar
vitamin
yoghurt

abstract painting
again
air-conditioning
anorak
back
clear (v.)
clothes
cycle (v.)
dinner
driver
face (make faces)
far
fine
freeway
fridge
Great!
hang out
healthy
Help yourself
human
hungry
life
news
nothing
picnic
rain (v.)
raw
ride (v.)
scratch
side
slice
someone
special
stare
starving
stop
sunny
thanks
treat
vegetarian

wake up
wave (v.)
weather
wildlife
yard

Unit 5

almost
artist
beautiful
best wishes
choose
co-presenter
crew (TV crew)
disc jockey
every
feature
first (at first)
fishing
FM signal
hear
introduce
local
mountain
next (Saturday)
own
particular
present (v.)
presenter
problem
programme
radio station
record (n.)
report (n.)
request (n.)
script
silly
song
successful
top
weak
work (v.)
world
year
youngest

Unit 6

Months and dates

Sports
athletics
badminton
baseball
basketball
football
golf
motor racing
squash
swimming
tennis

Sports locations
circuit
course
court
pitch

pool
track

baby
board
bored
breaststroke
certainly
chocolate
coach (= trainer)
compete
competition
crawl
crazy
difficult
dive
earn
easy (take it easy)
embarrassing
enjoy
event
fabulous
female
flavour
freak
friendly
fun
gate
goal
ground
hard
head
ice cream
jump (v.)
just
keen
kick off
later
length
live (opp. recorded)
lodge
lucky
magazine
match
middle of the road
mind (v.)
model (v.)
newspaper
own (on your own)
perfect
prefer
quality
queuing
reporter
right
rushing
score (v.)
secret
shopping
shout
signed
slowly
souvenir
spare (time)
stadium
star sign
straight

strawberry
strip (football)
supporter
suppose
Sure (= certainly)
take place
team
ticket
tomorrow
train (v.)
turn up
underwater
venue
well (as well)
well-known
where (rel. pron.)
which (rel. pron.)
who (rel. pron.)
wrong
Yuk!

Unit 7

School subjects

Common adjectives
awful/nice, good
big/small
boring/interesting
easy/difficult
expensive/cheap
heavy/light
late/early
old/young, new
slow/quick, fast
strong/weak
tall/short

ago
album
amazed
arrive
bad
barefoot
bet (v.)
brilliant
cab
completely
continue
cry (v.)
dark (dark blue)
die
dirty
doctor
doorstep
expect
explain
fever
find out
fine
follow
ghost
horse
hospital
ill
immediately

knock
life
lift (v.)
load (of rubbish)
long (How long?)
luckily
message
nearby
neck
passing
phone (v.)
pleased
pneumonia
point (v.)
pull
quite
recognise
recover
remember
result
save
scarf
score (n.)
shoe
smile
snow
somebody
start (v.)
stop (v.)
street
surgery
thank
train
treat
trousers
unconscious
up (What's up?)
upset
walk
website
winter
worried
year
yesterday

Unit 8

English money

Places in towns
art gallery
bus station
football stadium
hospital
ice rink
library
museum
night club
post office
railway station
swimming pool
theatre
tourist information office
town hall

appear
assistant
band
bass (guitar)
before
born
break up
buy
calendar
career
carpenter
change (= money)
charts
coin
college
creative
dance
denim
drummer
drums
ever
exactly
exhibition
fade
finally
follower
form (v.)
gift
gradually
happen
haircut
high point
hobby
hold
image
including
jacket
lead (guitar)
manager
married (get married)
nearly
noise
owner
packet
philosophy
postcard
rat
rhythm (guitar)
same
scream
sensation
single (n.)
straight ahead
sugar-free
suit (n.)
teens
together
tonight
turn
turning
value
way
weep
without

Unit 9

Rooms and parts of the house
balcony
bathroom
bedroom
dining room
garage
hall
kitchen
library
patio
pool
sitting room
study
toilet

Animals
budgie
cat
chicken
cow
crocodile
dog
duck
elephant
fox
giraffe
goat
goldfish
horse
kangaroo
koala bear
lamb
lion
parrot
pig
rabbit
rhinoceros
sheep
snake
spider
tiger

along
Alsatian dog
away
backwards
begin
birthday
blow (out)
candle
centimetre
crawl
cruel
danger
escape
extraordinary
farm
fear
feed
games arcade
grow
guess
Hands off!
inside
lake

ledge
narrow
open (*adj.*)
perhaps
pet
repay
rescue
reward
robbery
shout
smell (*v.*)
steak
strange
supermarket
supper
surprise
taste (*n.*)
wild (in the ...)
worst (fear the ...)

Unit 10

aggressive
alone
attack
back
badly
behind
bite (*n.* and *v.*)
bleed
blood
cloud
dinghy
enormous
face to face
fall off
fin
force
hand
harmless
hit
island
kilometre
leave
lose
mask
metre
photographer
protect
pygmy shark
reach
reef shark
rocket
roll
row (a boat)
shoulder
snorkel
somewhere
species
suddenly
surface
through
towards
whale shark

Unit 11

Materials
cotton
gold
leather
metal
nylon
plastic
silk
silver
wood (wooden)
wool (woollen)

Personal possessions
bag
bracelet
buckle
chain
diary
keyring
pencil case
personal stereo
purse
rucksack
scarf
strap
wallet
watch

Clothes
belt
boots
cardigan
dress
jacket
jeans
pullover
shirt
shoes
skirt
sweater
sweatshirt
T-shirt
top
trainers
trousers

Style of clothes
baggy
long/short sleeved
tight

Hair colour and style
blonde
brown
curly
dark
fair
long
short
wavy

Regular and irregular past participles

At last!
campsite
contact
day trip
hand (something) in
hang on
last (*adv.*)
Let's get going!
lose
moon
need
Never mind
pass (*v.*)
put
scooter
search (*v.*)
spare
star
sticker
stuff
swap
touch (in touch)

Unit 12

Adjectives of measurement
fast
heavy
high
long
wide

acceleration
bad –worse –worst
before (*adv.*)
bungee jumping
candyfloss
comfort (*v.*)
dangerous
details
drink (*v.*)
duration
earth
estate (car)
experience (*v.*)
far –further –furthest
few
frightened
frightening
funny
good –better –best
hatchback
head (of a corporation)
height
helicopter
horrible
interrupt
jet fighter plane
last (*adj.*)
length
make (*n.*)
of course not
paragliding
play (*n.*)
popular

price
reliable
ride (*n.*)
rollercoaster
safe (*adj.*)
safety
seat
second (*n.*)
sick
similar
speed
sports car
suit (Suit yourself!)
take off
taste (*n.* and *v.*)
technical
terrifying
theme park
thrill
track
ultimate
weight
whitewater rafting
width

Unit 13

Parts of the body
ankle
arm
back
ear
elbow
eye
face
finger
foot (*pl.* feet)
hair
hand
head
hip
knee
leg
mouth
neck
nose
shoulder
stomach
teeth (*sing.* tooth)
thumb
toe
waist
wrist

accident
almost
bandage
bin
body
carry
compress
cut
dark (*n.*)
date (go out on)
dress (*v.*)
drop
earrings

faint
farmhouse
full stop
gloves
hat
hurt
ice pack
idea
important
keep up
kiss (*v.*)
laugh at
lie
lift (*n.*)
lipstick
litter
look out
looks
manners
matter (*v.*)
mistake
nicely
old-fashioned
painful
part
path
pay (*v.*)
plaster
polite
probably
race track
raise
rest (*v.*)
ribbon
ring (*n.*)
scar
share (*n.*)
sprain
stand up
Stone Age
tease
tie (*n.*)
tights
turn on (the light)
twist
view

Unit 14

Household jobs
clear the table
do the cleaning
do the cooking
do the ironing
do the shopping
do the vacuuming
do the washing
do the washing-up
make the bed
tidy up

Occupations
beautician
carpenter
cashier
cleaner
dentist
doctor

electrician
engineer
hairdresser
nurse
plumber
receptionist
sales assistant
secretary
waiter

Bad luck!
believe
blouse
business
collect
collection
delivery
empty (v.)
entrance
explosion
full-time
housework
huff (in a huff)
navy blue
nerves (gets on my nerves)
office
parcel
park (n.)
perfume
plant
play group
post (v.)
refuse (v.)
rubbish
salon
serve
shelf (pl. shelves)
smell (n.)
sort (v.)
sound (v.)
stamp (v.)
toy
trolley
uniform
untidy
waste (of time)
water
work experience

Unit 15

advise
agree
amount
babysitting
billion
button
company
consultant
dollar
employ
equipment
fashion
focus group
hire
however
imaginary

in (= fashionable)
kid
multinational
notebook
notice
opinion
out (= unfashionable)
pocket
pocket money
product
research project
secure
sense
software
specialist
strongly
style – stylish
survey
tape recorder

Unit 16

Leisure activities

barbecue
beach
bowling
circus
concert
go-karting
ice-skating
line-skating
picnic
sailing
sightseeing

acrobat
acrobatics
advice
African
artist
Caribbean
carnival
classic
demand
different
disappointed
display
end (n.)
exercise (= physical activity)
festival
fight (v.)
hero
inspired by
Latin American
list
magician
middle (n.)
musical (n.)
once-in-a-lifetime
opportunity
orchestra
parade
performed by
prefer
rather (I'd rather)
sad
smart

spectacular
view (on view)
What's on?

Unit 17

Adjectives and adverbs

angry – angrily
background
beautiful(ly)
beg
blow (I've blown it)
bus shelter
busy
capital
careful(ly)
careless(ly)
catch
certain
chance
check
complain
completely
curtains
difference
dry cleaner's
emergency
engaged (tone on phone)
expert
fresh air
get off (the streets)
instructions
lady
living (make a ...)
loud(ly)
medical
miss (v.)
normal
organisation
pavement
persuade
put up
quiet(ly)
regularly
salesman
shelter
society
soft toy
steal
sweets
terrible – terribly
trade
trust
unhappy
unpaid
voluntary work

Unit 18

Jobs in the media

actor / actress
camera operator
director
journalist
make-up artist

scriptwriter
sound engineer

Types of film

action
cartoon
comedy
disaster
gangster
historical
horror
love story
musical
science fiction
thriller
western

abroad
add
advance (in ...)
android
autograph
battle
character
correct
couple
desert
design
destroy
develop
drown
episode
evil (adj. and n.)
forever
galaxy
good (n.)
guide (n.)
iceberg
knight
land (v.)
mercenary
order (n.)
over (many times over)
passenger
pilot
planet
power
producer
promise (v.)
recently
record (v.)
record-breaking
restore
rule
scene
security badge
separate (adj.)
set (= location)
set (the alarm)
shot
soap opera
spaceship
special effects
storyline
studio
switch off
team up with

Unit 19

Food and drink
(See also Unit 4)
drink (soft drink)
fish cake
lemonade
mineral water
orange juice
pie
scampi
soup
sparkling
vanilla

abolish
alcohol
American
anniversary
assassinate
assemble
Atlantic
board (on board)
box
build
canal
cloth
coast
commit (suicide)
compose
conditions
construct
copper
crown
customs
deck
destination
disease
dish
divided
exercise (v.)
exchange
extremely
flight
force (v.)
friendship
glass (adj.)
goods
gun
harbour
huge
hurry
illegal
independence
inner
invent
involve
landmark
liberty
lie down
lottery
main course
Morse Code
ocean
overboard
pedestal
period
point (n.)

pronunciation
pyramid
represent
room (= space)
route
sculptor
section
sell
separate (v.)
side order
solo
spike
stand
state
statue
structure
suicide
symbol
throw
token
trader
transatlantic
triangular
trouble
unusual
viewing gallery
visitor
voyage

Unit 20

anger
apartment
bathe
bomb (v.)
calm
celebrate
cellar
childhood
comfortable
country
hill
hope (n.)
jug
lawyer
nervous
peace
pick someone up (= give someone a lift)
politician
practise
precious
publish
remain
remarkable
sheet
shell (v.)
shelling
shut down
sincerely
thought (n.)
typical
war

Irregular verbs

Infinitive	Past simple	Past participle
be	was	been
become	became	become
begin	began	begun
bite	bit	bitten
blow	blew	blown
break	broke	broken
bring	brought	brought
build	built	built
buy	bought	bought
catch	caught	caught
choose	chose	chosen
come	came	come
cost	cost	cost
cut	cut	cut
do	did	done
draw	drew	drawn
drink	drank	drunk
drive	drove	driven
eat	ate	eaten
fall	fell	fallen
feed	fed	fed
feel	felt	felt
fight	fought	fought
find	found	found
fly	flew	flown
forget	forgot	forgotten
get	got	got
give	gave	given
go	went	gone
grow	grew	grown
have	had	had
hear	heard	heard
hit	hit	hit
hold	held	held
hurt	hurt	hurt
keep	kept	kept
know	knew	known
learn	learnt	learnt
leave	left	left
lend	lent	lent
lose	lost	lost
make	made	made
meet	met	met
pay	paid	paid
put	put	put
read	read	read
ride	rode	ridden
ring	rang	rung
run	ran	run
say	said	said
see	saw	seen
sell	sold	sold
send	sent	sent

Infinitive	Past simple	Past participle
shine	shone	shone
shut	shut	shut
sing	sang	sung
sit	sat	sat
sleep	slept	slept
speak	spoke	spoken
spend	spent	spent
split up	split up	split up
stand	stood	stood
steal	stole	stolen
swim	swam	swum
take	took	taken
teach	taught	taught
tell	told	told
think	thought	thought
throw	threw	thrown
understand	understood	understood
wake (up)	woke (up)	woken (up)
wear	wore	worn
weep	wept	wept
win	won	won
write	wrote	written